A Guide to
CULTS
& New Religions

Ronald Enroth & Others

InterVarsity Press
Downers Grove
Illinois 60515

InterVarsity Press is the book-publishing division of Inter-Varsity Christian Fellowship, a student movement active on campus at hundreds of universities, colleges and schools of nursing. For information about local and regional activities, write IVCF, 233 Langdon St., Madison, WI 53703.

Distributed in Canada through InterVarsity Press, 860 Denison St., Unit 3, Markham, Ontario L3R 4H1, Canada.

Biblical quotations in chapter two, "The Baha'i Faith," are from the New English Bible, copyright © The Delegates of the Oxford University Press and the Syndics of the Cambridge University Press 1961, 1970. Reprinted by permission.

Biblical quotations in chapter eight, "Latter-day Saints," are from the Authorized (King James) Version.

Biblical quotations marked NIV are taken from the Holy Bible: New International Version, copyright © 1978 by the New York International Bible Society. Used by permission of Zondervan Bible Publishers.

Biblical quotations marked NASB are from the New American Standard Bible.

All other biblical quotations are from the Revised Standard Version of the Bible, copyrighted 1946, 1952, © 1971, 1973, and are used by permission.

Chapter four, "Eckankar," was revised and reprinted by permission of the Spiritual Counterfeits Project, Inc., © 1979, P.O. Box 2418, Berkeley, CA 94702.

ISBN 0-87784-837-8

Printed in the United States of America

Library of Congress Cataloging in Publication Data

Enroth, Ronald M.
    A guide to cults and new religions.

    Bibliography: p.
    Contents: Baha'i–Bhagwan Shree Rajneesh–
Eckankar– [etc.]
        1. Cults–United States.   2. Sects–United States.
 I. Title.
BL2530.U6E57   1983   291   83-44
    ISBN 0-87784-837-8

18	17	16	15	14	13	12	11	10	9	8	7	6	5	4	3	2	1
97	96	95	94	93	92	91	90	89	88	87		86	85	84	83		

1. **What Is a Cult?** ——————————————————9
   Ronald Enroth
2. **The Baha'i Faith** ——————————————25
   John Boykin
3. **Bhagwan Shree Rajneesh** ————————————43
   Eckart Floether with Eric Pement
4. **Eckankar** ———————————————————59
   Mark Albrecht, Brooks Alexander & Woodrow Nichols
5. **est** ——————————————————————75
   John Weldon
6. **Hare Krishna (ISKCON)** ———————————91
   J. Isamu Yamamoto
7. **Jehovah's Witnesses** ——————————————103
   Wesley Walters & Kurt Goedelman
8. **Latter-day Saints (Mormons)** ——————————117
   Donald S. Tingle
9. **Transcendental Meditation** ————————————135
   David Haddon
10. **Unification Church (Moonies)** ——————————151
    J. Isamu Yamamoto
11. **The Way** ————————————————————173
    Joel MacCollam
12. **Evaluating Cults and New Religions** ——————191
    LaVonne Neff
Notes ————————————————————————199
Reading List ——————————————————————214
About the Authors ——————————————————216

Preface

People today are spiritually starving. Western society is now almost totally secularized—little satisfaction for spiritual hunger can be found in its institutions. Even the Christian church, in many cases, has lost sight of the meat and drink of God's words. The result is that many who "hunger and thirst for righteousness" remain unfilled, craving food but not knowing where to find it.

Enter the cults and new religions. Spin-offs of orthodox religions—Christianity, Islam, Eastern religions—or of traditional psychology, these groups offer purpose, hope and spiritual nourishment. Many young people are quite willing to try to meet their needs in these new religious groups.

A Guide to Cults and New Religions surveys ten such groups and compares their teachings with those of biblical Christianity. The ten groups chosen are not necessarily the largest or the most active, but they represent the spectrum of new religions: groups with Western, Eastern and Middle-Eastern roots; groups that grew out of Christianity and groups that have no resemblance at all to it; groups that sprang up a few years ago and groups that have become American institutions.

Inclusion or exclusion of any group does not imply a judgment: we have tried to offer a representative sampling of cults and new religions, not an exhaustive encyclopedia. Readers who study these groups will be able to apply what they have learned to other, similar groups.

The opening chapter, "What Is a Cult?" discusses characteristics common to most new religions, and the final chapter, "Evaluating Cults and New Religions," gives principles that can help in understanding any religious group. Our intention throughout has been not so much to give the Christian answer to every possible challenge as to present guidelines that can be applied to an unending variety of situations.

Most chapters in this book were originally published as small booklets and are available from InterVarsity Press, Box F, Downers Grove, IL 60515. Since cults and new religions are constantly growing and changing, however, each chapter has been updated.

Because this book will be read selectively, we have asked the authors to present the kernel of the Christian message in each chapter. Our goal, after all, is not to discredit cults and new religions but to present the good news of Jesus, "the power of God for salvation to every one who has faith" (Rom 1:16).

The Publisher

1

What Is a Cult?

Ronald Enroth

IN A MIDWESTERN SUBURB A RELIGIOUS organization called Eckankar had scheduled an informational meeting for the public in the community room of a local bank. Following the publication of a story in a major local newspaper describing Eckankar as a "religious cult," the bank changed its mind and withdrew its approval of the use of the room by the group. "We weren't aware they were considered a cult," explained the bank's branch manager.

"We are not a cult," countered a spokesperson for the group who reportedly objected to his group's placement on a list of cults. "I guess we're on the list because we're not Christian, and when you're not Christian, you're going to find a group of conservative Christians who cannot tolerate anything different in society."

Eckankar, "the ancient science of soul travel," defines itself as the oldest religious teaching known to man. In a letter expressing concern over my use of the designation *cult* in connection with Eckankar, its Director of Spiritual Services told me that his organization is "unlike any other teaching in the world today. It does not fit into any category.... Members of ECKANKAR are some of the most well-liked people in our society.... ECKANKAR is in no way a cult, but simply an ancient teaching brought out to the modern world."

An interesting footnote to this account, no doubt unknown to most Eckists, is the fact that Eckankar's founder and one-time leader referred to his own organization as "a one man cult, with myself as founder, president and disciple."[1]

In short, depending on whom you talk to (or read), Eckankar is a cult or not a cult at all.

A similar problem developed in the fall of 1980 after an article entitled "A Bad Karma on Main Line" appeared in a Philadelphia newspaper.[2] It was a story about the Church Universal and Triumphant and its efforts to establish a branch in the Philadelphia area. The group's leader, Elizabeth Clare Prophet (affectionately known as "Guru Ma"), and its members were identified as cultists who engaged in strange rituals and mindless chanting.

In a strongly worded letter of response, a leader of the Church Universal and Triumphant decried the use of the word *cult*, claiming it invites the reader "to dismiss our church and its teachings as a group which obviously would have no credibility to any thinking person. We categorically reject the pejorative label, 'cult.' We are a responsible church."[3]

These two illustrations typify numerous examples which could be cited to indicate the confusion, disagreement and emotion surrounding the word *cult*. What is a cult? The definition varies, of course, with the frame of reference of the person making it.

To the sixteenth-century Roman Catholic, Lutheranism was a cult. To first-century Judaism, the Christian church was a cult in that it deviated from prevailing orthodoxy. To some contemporary Jews, the evangelical organization Jews for Jesus is a cult. Cult researchers Flo Conway and Jim Siegelman have indirectly linked

Campus Crusade for Christ (and "born-again Christianity" in general) with cultic behavior.

Academicians and other respected cult watchers disagree on the usage and meaning of terms like *sect* and *cult*. Academic usage of such labels is both more precise and more technical than their use in everyday parlance. That does not mean, however, that either clarity or consensus has been achieved.

In a footnote to an article which he wrote for a learned journal, sociologist Thomas Robbins noted that the term *cult* is increasingly applied "to a disparate collection of groups and movements, and consequently has become unsuitable as a precise legal or social scientific category. . . . In effect, a 'cult' is any group stigmatized as a 'cult.' "[4]

In addition to the terms *cult* and *sect,* various experts and academic commentators have used designations like "unconventional religions," "emergent religions," "non-normative religions," "marginal religious movements" and, most frequently, "new religious movements" to refer to new and nontraditional religious groups.

Regarding the alternative definitions of *cult,* Brooks Alexander has observed: "Such confusion is perhaps inevitable when a term that is essentially religious in derivation is appropriated by analysts who have no religious stance or standard of their own. Under the circumstances, we are entitled to ask if the word has not lost its usefulness and usability altogether."[5]

Although the word *cult* has become a blurred designation, it will undoubtedly continue to receive wide use. Its negative connotations are inescapable, especially since Jonestown. No one wants to be identified as a member of a cult. Given the various meanings surrounding the word and the admission by some that its usefulness has been diminished, should we stop using it? James Sire's brief response to that question perhaps says it best: "We should if we could, but we can't. . . . I think we are stuck with it."[6]

With this in mind, a closer examination of the concept of cult is in order. We should first note that the original use of the word as well as its more technical academic application today derives from the Latin *cultus*, "worship." In this sense the cultic act is an act of worship, involving external rites and ceremonies as well as attitudes of reverential homage. A popularized version of this understanding of cult can be seen in our reference to personality cults. For example, we speak of an Elvis Presley cult or a Hitler cult involving a form of homage or devotion to a particular person.

A related common usage of the word *cult* is illustrated in the following excerpt from the sports section of a West Coast newspaper: "There's a cult meeting scheduled for East Beach Sunday. Over 12,000 believers are expected to attend, and they'll be joined by television crews from three local network affiliates. There'll be hero worshiping, ritual and revelry—all the ingredients of a cult classic." What is being described is California's volleyball cult, and the kind of "worship" that takes place at such an event is common to sports fans everywhere. (Interestingly, the word *fan* derives from *fanatic*, another term frequently associated with religious extremism or cultism.)

Definitions of Cults

One could take at least three approaches in defining *cult*: a sensational or popular approach, a sociological approach and a theological approach. A sensational approach to cults is built on journalistic accounts in the popular press which frequently focus on the dramatic and sometimes bizarre aspects of cultic behavior. A sociological definition includes the authoritarian, manipulative, totalistic and sometimes communal features of cults. A theological definition involves some standard of orthodoxy.

Let's consider each of these three approaches to sample the diversity of perspectives before offering any tentative response to the question, What is a cult? It will soon be apparent that any simple and precise attempt to delineate a cult must be viewed with caution, if not suspicion, because of the common tendency to oversimplify a very complex phenomenon.

Most people gain an image of what cults are and how they

operate through the news media. Journalists are frequently required to sacrifice in-depth research and careful analysis in favor of a story that sells, a story with human interest appeal. Cults often provide exotic material for the media. Accounts of bizarre behavior, including mysterious rites, promiscuous sex, occult practices and robes of white sackcloth, make for good copy. As a result, when the public thinks of cults, the images conjured up include flower-pinning Hare Krishnas at airports, zombielike followers of a Korean evangelist who claims to have talked with Jesus and Buddha in the spirit world, and orange-robed disciples of a guru named Rajneesh cavorting in a cosmic encounter group.

On the other hand, new religious movements like Eckankar remain largely unknown to the public because of their lower visibility and minimal media value, despite the fact that their membership is considerably larger than that of better-known groups like the Moonies and the Hare Krishnas.

Popular and often sensationalized descriptions of cults tend to play up such adjectives as "strange," "curious" and "unconventional." The fact is, however, that many new cults and sects *are* alien to the average person in the West. Many are Eastern imports with unfamiliar spiritual technology including chanting, meditation and various forms of yoga. Such practices, despite their growing acceptance in the West, still represent non-normative behavior vis-à-vis established religion.

The Judeo-Christian mainstream denominations have established themselves; that is, they have persisted for generations and have become acceptable, respectable and traditional parts of the religious landscape of North America. Many of the "new" religious movements are not new at all; some, in fact, antedate Christianity. However, they are strangers to *these* shores. They are considered strange and curious because they are unconventional. The larger society views them with suspicion and anxiety in much the same way that the American mainstream population received newly arrived ethnic groups during the era of mass immigration. They generate an aura of unfamiliarity.

Sociologists define cultic religion in order to locate it in its wider social context. A sociological approach to understanding cults will necessarily involve comparative and historical dimensions. Sociologists examine each movement in the light of information derived from the study of other movements, both past and present. They wish to identify, in an objective manner, patterns of psychosocial behavior that seem to characterize all or most groups under discussion.

From a sociological perspective, there are important differences between the categories *church* and *sect* or *cult*. Churches are culture-accepting religious organizations; that is, they have accommodated in varying degrees to the dominant cultural and social realities. Sects and cults, in contrast, are culture rejecting. Not only are their belief systems typically outside the Judeo-Christian tradition, but these groups usually exhibit great alienation from other dominant social structures and the prevailing culture. In the words of sociologist John Lofland, cults are "little groups" which break off from the "conventional consensus and espouse very different views of the real, the possible, and the moral."[7]

Because cultic world views are, by definition, quite different from the dominant cultural perspective, we should expect that new religious movements will experience difficulties as they engage in recruitment of new members, fundraising, indoctrination efforts and other aspects of their involvement in the often disapproving parent society. The sociologist, aware that the term *cult* retains disparaging implications, is interested in the social dynamics that relate to the labeling process as these groups interact with the larger society.

A comprehensive sociological definition of cult would include consideration of such factors as authoritarian leadership patterns, loyalty and commitment mechanisms, lifestyle characteristics, conformity patterns (including the use of various sanctions in connection with those members who deviate) and the many other features common to sectarian, elitist religious groups.

For the Christian the most significant component of a definition of cult is theological in nature. This is so because basic issues of truth and error are involved. Unlike the secular sociologist who is unconcerned about the truth of a particular belief and unlike the typical person whose religious naiveté precludes any serious interest in doctrinal matters, the Christian must be able to distinguish truth from error.

A theological definition of cult must be based on a standard of Christian orthodoxy. Using the Bible's teaching as a focal point, James W. Sire defines a cult as "any religious movement that is organizationally distinct and has doctrines and/or practices that contradict those of the Scriptures as interpreted by traditional Christianity as represented by the major Catholic and Protestant denominations, and as expressed in such statements as the Apostles' Creed."[8]

A theological analysis of a particular group's belief system would examine issues like the group's understanding of the person and work of Jesus Christ, its view of human nature and sin, its teaching regarding salvation, the Trinity, and the nature and role of the Bible, as well as many other questions crucial to the historic position of orthodoxy.

James Bjornstad reminds us that in today's supermarket of religious diversity, the counterfeits of biblical Christianity are well disguised. He observes that "members of unorthodox religious groups often use the same terms Christians use. They ... reinterpret statements of doctrine and biblical passages. They ... seek to overwhelm with false scholarship. They might even willingly deceive or not reveal their whole theology."[9] One such Christian counterfeit is The Way, whose founder, Victor Paul Wierwille, proclaims, "Jesus Christ is not God, never was and never will be." This view is echoed by the United Pentecostal Church (or the Oneness movement), which describes the doctrine of the Trinity as "the most diabolical religious hoax and scandal in history."

Although they are sometimes reluctant to discuss it publicly, members of the Reverend Moon's Unification Church believe that

Moon is the Messiah, the Lord of the Second Advent. Within the movement he and his wife are known as the True Parents. In a highly sacred rite of the church presided over by Moon and known as the Holy Wine Ceremony, members are told that they are being "grafted to" the True Parents. As they receive the cup of holy wine, they are told by Moon himself, "You are going to be transformed into members of the heavenly family and belong directly to the True Parents, and thus directly to God. . . . By taking this holy wine you will be instantly changed into descendants of God."[10]

In a talk to participants in a holy wine ceremony, a top leader of the Moonies made the following revealing statement: "We members of the Unification Church are living in another Messianic era. We are a privileged people who have known the True Parents of mankind. We are privileged people who are allowed to see God, not in a mirror dimly, but face to face. . . . We shall pledge our lives to God and the True Parents."[11]

It is clear from such statements how members of the Unification Church view Moon and why the doctrines of his church have been called heretical by both liberal and conservative Christians. While this cult's recruitment tactics and political-economic activities deserve our attention and analysis, the key problem and focal concern for the Christian must be the group's aberrant theology.

Again, of all the approaches to defining a cult, the theological or doctrinal is the one least addressed by secular analysts. The lack of interest in such matters is typified by a statement by the distinguished sociologist of religion, Bryan Wilson. "The sociologist is not concerned to test the 'truth' of belief. He is not concerned with the efficacy of rituals. He does not attempt to judge between divergent interpretations of a tradition. He does not challenge the claimed legitimation for practices and ideas which religionists endorse."[12]

From the Christian perspective, however, categories of truth and falsehood do not indicate a constricted fundamentalist mentality but are crucial to retaining a posture of orthodoxy. "We must affirm the proposition that God has revealed himself in the person of his Son, Jesus Christ, and that his Word, the Bible, serves as the only baseline for comparison when ascertaining truth and error. After all, what really matters is not a label of 'conventional' or 'unconventional' religion, but God's objective truth."[13]

While secularists may exhibit disdain for the theological side of the cult question, evangelical Christians have been guilty of focusing almost exclusively on doctrinal/theological concerns and have neglected the psychosocial aberrations of cults. As one concerned Christian layman put it (without suggesting that we abandon a theological critique of the cults), "I think there is merit for placing more stress on the other danger zones created by the cults, such as psychological and moral injury, disruption of family ties, impairment of scholastic and professional careers."[14] A more encompassing definition of what constitutes cultism would contribute to more effective rehabilitation as well as evangelization of those persons caught up in aberrational religious groups.

With these assumptions in mind, let's examine more fully some of the characteristics of cults, drawing on the various perspectives suggested above. A holistic approach to cults will surely include sociological and theological features and may well contain descriptive elements which are exotic, even bizarre.

Characteristics of Cults

Whether we are theologians or sociologists, philosophers or readers of the morning paper, when we hear the word *cult* we think of certain distinguishing marks. What features can we expect to find in most cults? We will look at nine common characteristics. All cults have some of these features; not all cults have all of them.

1. *Authoritarian.* A crucial dimension of all cultic organizations is authoritarian leadership. There is always a central, charismatic (in the personality sense), living human leader who commands total loyalty and allegiance. Tangible evidence of the leaders' significance can be seen in their titles: "Apostle" (John Robert Stevens) of the Church of the Living Word, informally known as "The Walk"; "Perfect Master" (Guru Maharaj Ji) of the

Divine Light Mission; "Father David" (Mo Berg) of the Children of God; "Mother of the Universe" and "Messenger for the Great White Brotherhood" (Elizabeth Clare Prophet) of the Church Universal and Triumphant; "Master" and "True Parent" (Moon) of the Unification Church.

The leader exercises authority over both doctrine and practice, and his/her interpretations of the "truth" are accepted by the members without question. The members' self-identity and life goals are redefined and have meaning only in relation to the leader and the group. Moon once told a group of followers: "Father [referring to himself] is telling you all this this morning because ... he wants you to become a part of him, part of Sun Myung Moon." On a similar occasion Moon proclaimed: "You are now entitled to being loved by the True Parents by being loyal to them. . . . You must do anything and everything instructed by the True Parents."

2. *Oppositional.* Robert Ellwood speaks of the "oppositional stance, style and substance" of the new cult movements.[15] Their beliefs, practices and values are counter to those of the dominant culture. They often place themselves in an adversarial role vis-à-vis major social institutions. The Church of Scientology, for example, engages in an almost constant series of attacks on the government. Scientologists feel that they are being persecuted by various government agencies.

Perhaps the social institution most affected by the oppositional stance of the cults is the family. The most outspoken critics of the new religious movements are parents who have experienced the often painful distancing and separation from their children that occur when young people join extremist groups.

Moon has described his church's efforts as a "tug of war to win young people." Speaking of himself he says: "Father came to America and began to pull her young people toward the side of God. This has produced a great deal of commotion."[16]

3. *Exclusivistic.* Related to the oppositional character of cults is their elitism and exclusionism. The group is the only one which

possesses the "truth," and therefore to leave the group is to endanger one's salvation. Usually the new "truth" is based on a new revelation given to the group's prophet/ founder/leader. Victor Paul Wierwille of The Way believes that God spoke to him audibly and promised to help him teach the Word as it had not been taught since the first century.

A former member of an aberrational Christian group describes the attitude of exclusiveness so typical of the cultic mind set. "Our leader was critical of all established denominational churches and all people who didn't believe as he taught. I became mentally isolated because it was felt that nobody outside of Glory Barn teaching was walking in as much truth as we were and therefore their opinion was not valid. I became cloistered in a world of Bible meetings and spiritual pride. I felt that I had all the right truth and that no other people had anything to offer."

4. *Legalistic.* Tightly structured autocratic groups operate within a legalistic framework which governs both spiritual matters and the details of everyday living. Rules and regulations abound. The specifics of a member's life are controlled by policies and procedures originating with the leadership. Sometimes these strictures apply to outside visitors. The Christ Family, for example, believing that killing animals as well as eating meat and wearing leather is wrong, requires visitors to take off their belts and shoes before entering one of its camps.

It is not unusual for cults to dictate mode of dress, length of hair and the type of personal adornment permitted, if any. Even those groups not readily identifiable by distinctive dress or other religious insignia do regulate some aspects of their members' outward appearance. For example, the Church Universal and Triumphant, a highly occult/psychic group, recommends jewelry that is gold, gold-plated or gold-filled. "Copper or silver jewelry is not worn as it conducts the lower rather than the higher vibrations of the self." Students at Summit University, an institution operated by the cult, are told that "neither the eyes nor the third eye should be covered with hair in either men or women." The students' *Code of Conduct* further states: "Since hair carries the records of the past, both men and women are encouraged to have short hair at Summit University as part of the alchemy of the new birth—a sign of non-attachment and of willing self-sacrifice."[17]

5. *Subjective.* Cultic movements place considerable emphasis on the experiential—on feelings and emotions. This is especially true of the new age psychotherapies and self-improvement groups like est and Lifespring. "Follow your feelings" is the message of Rajneesh and many other contemporary gurus. For Rajneesh, life is a cosmic joke. "My religion is rooted in playfulness, in nonseriousness."[18]

Many young adults are attracted to new age groups because of the appeal of subjective experience. A devotee of Guru Maharaj Ji describes his initial reaction to Divine Light Mission recruiters: "I don't really remember their words, but just the feeling I got from them. It was really blissful."

Subjectivism is sometimes linked to anti-intellectualism, putting down rational processes and devaluing knowledge and education. The anti-intellectual mentality is clearly illustrated in this bit of advice to young people from "Apostle" Stevens of The Walk: "Stay away from Bible schools.... We can produce better ministers with our eyes blindfolded than the seminaries can."[19]

6. *Persecution-Conscious.* Perceived persecution is one of the hallmarks of virtually all new religious movements. Their literature, public statements and in-house indoctrination all convey the theme that in one form or another their group is being singled out for persecution—by mainstream Christians, the press, parents or the government.

Yogi Bhajan, leader of 3HO (Healthy Happy Holy Organization), comments: "The critics didn't spare Jesus Christ, they didn't spare Buddha, and they don't spare me."[20] When Moon was indicted on federal tax evasion charges in 1981, he told a group of followers that he was declaring war on "the real enemies of America" and interpreted the U.S. government's action against him as prejudicial. He reminded his audience that the Unification Church is "an oppressed minority in America" and stated that he "would not be standing here today if my skin were white and my religion were Presbyterian."[21]

In a publication interestingly titled *The Truth,* a small aberrational Christian sect known variously as "The Truth Station" and "The River of Life Ministry" complained that use of the word *cult* was unfair and merely an "end-time strategy" of Satan. "Subtly, misunderstanding and persecution are mounting against righteous believers, exactly as it was when Christ walked on the earth.... True believers are being called 'cultists.' "[22]

7. *Sanction-Oriented.* Cults require conformity to established practices and beliefs and readily exercise sanctions against the wayward. Those who fail to demonstrate the proper allegiance, who raise too many questions, disobey the rules or openly rebel are punished, formally excommunicated or merely asked to leave the group.

Various control mechanisms are used to insure conformity. The more extreme cults regularly employ fear, intimidation and guilt to manipulate members. Frequently members are inculcated with the fear that something terrible will happen to them or their loved ones should they ever leave the group. "Rebellious" people are sometimes subjected to emotional public confessions and humiliation, including physical "rebukes" like slapping. The signing of covenants and loyalty oaths is another means to achieve control.

8. *Esoteric.* Cultic religion is a religion of secrecy and concealment. Eastern spirituality, especially, has been described by Brooks Alexander as "split-level religion, with an *inner truth* (the real truth) and an *outer truth* (an appealing, but limited and somewhat misleading face)." This kind of esotericism, Alexander continues, "accepts the appropriateness (and practical necessity) of a deliberately created gap between the picture that is projected to the general public and the inner reality known to initiates."[23]

This esoteric gap also characterizes some aberrant groups adhering to the margins of Christianity. A former member of such a group discovered levels of secrecy within the organization.

Cassette tapes and public sermons were always carefully edited. "After one is there for a while, partaking of the surface services and sermons, one is then introduced to what is termed the 'deeper truths' at special teaching meetings."

Members of the Church Universal and Triumphant who receive that group's secret "Keepers of the Flame Lessons" are required to sign a statement saying, in part: "I shall keep the trust that is placed in me by keeping the lessons confidential, sharing them with no one. And I shall see to it that the lessons are either burned or returned to you upon my transition from this plane." That is the quintessence of esotericism.

9. *Antisacerdotal.* Cults tend to be organizations comprised of lay people. There are no paid clergy or professional religious functionaries like those in traditional groups. That is not to say that cults do not have spiritual hierarchies or titles applying to specific roles, such as *shepherd, mahatma, chela, baba, swami* or *prophet.*

It is important to remember that antisacerdotal groups stress the involvement of everyone; the opportunities extend to all; each member has equal access to the truth. Bryan Wilson points out that this opposition to clergy "arises from the need of the inspirators of these movements to legitimize their own departure from prevailing orthodoxy—an orthodoxy warranted and sustained by the claims of a priestly class."[24]

Not surprisingly, antisacerdotal cults often choose not to hold their religious observances in the kinds of buildings usually associated with traditional religions. Instead, they meet in "centers," "meeting halls," private homes, meditation rooms and, in at least one case, a barn.

Categories of Cults

We have seen that the term *cult* provides a useful handle, a way of identifying a complex set of behaviors and characteristics in a single concept. In order to make sense out of the diversity of cults and new religious movements, it is helpful to place the groups into various categories. Professor Bryan Wilson identifies cults as world-denying, world-indifferent or world-enhancing.[25]

World-denying cults emphasize the evilness of the world system and the necessity to be saved *from* the world. They tend to remove their followers from the larger society and to develop separate, communal (though not monastic) lifestyles. Groups illustrating this kind of cult are the Children of God, the Hare Krishna movement, the Christ Family, the Alamo Christian Foundation and the Church of Armageddon (also known as the Love Family).

World-indifferent cults tolerate the secular society while at the same time encouraging their believers to seek a purer, more spiritual life within the world, attempting to be *in* the world while not being *of* the world. Members associate primarily with each other but usually do not establish a separate communal existence. They engage in normal "worldly" activities such as holding jobs and obtaining educations. Examples include The Way International, the Self-Realization Fellowship, some members of the Unification Church and aberrational Christian groups like The Walk.

World-enhancing cults include those groups—many of which are quasi-religious or claim to be nonreligious (like TM)—consciously seeking to improve the skills and well-being of their members, thus purportedly enhancing their enjoyment of and participation in the larger society. Although some of these groups claim a social conscience (as in est's involvement in The Hunger Project), the ultimate goal is self-transformation and self-improvement. Included here are the Church of Scientology, TM, est, Lifespring and PSI World.

Another classificatory scheme is outlined in my book *The Lure of the Cults.* It describes five basic categories of new religious movements: (1) Eastern mystical, (2) aberrational Christian, (3) psychospiritual or self-improvement, (4) eclectic-syncretistic, and (5) psychic-occult-astral.[26] When dealing with all the religious groups today subsumed under the term *cult*—at least in evangelical Christian circles—a sixth category is necessary: institutionalized or established groups, including Jehovah's Witnesses, Mormons, Christian Science, Unity School of Christianity, etc.

Whatever system of classification is used or whatever list of cultic traits is enumerated, there will always be gaps, inadequacies, overlaps and even inconsistencies. In the final analysis, each cult is unique and requires specific and careful study.

Both Christian and secular cult analysts need to beware the tendency to use overgeneralized stereotypes regarding new religious movements. Robbins and Anthony describe the "generic fallacy" of assuming that "properties imputed to one notorious 'cult' necessarily apply to other unconventional or controversial groups, or that all such movements are basically similar."[27]

It is true from a strictly academic perspective that the label *cult* may oversimplify a complex phenomenon and tend to obscure important differences among cultic groups. Nevertheless, the Christian observer must always recognize the basic pattern of evil and false teaching which is an unmistakable theme in all groups departing from God's revealed truth. For "as long as the secular analysts ignore God's consistent proclamation that humanity is fallen and living in alienation from God and is in need of reconciliation through the only reigning Lord, Jesus Christ, they will continue to put band-aids on broken arms."[28]

2

The Baha'i Faith

John Boykin

*The unity of nations ... in this century will
be securely established, causing all
the peoples of the world to regard themselves as
citizens of one common fatherland.*
Abdu'l-Baha

ON COLLEGE CAMPUSES MEMBERS of the Baha'i Faith sponsor Baha'i clubs, information tables and Baha'i weeks, with lectures, visiting professors and concerts. Rock superstars Seals and Crofts weave Baha'i symbolism into their songs and present the Faith to their concert audiences. Attractive signs in airports show the Baha'i Temple in Wilmette, Illinois, along with messages of peace and brotherhood.

The Baha'i Faith brings a message of Unity: all religions are one, true science and true religion are one, all peoples are one. Baha'is advocate equality for men and women, a universal language and abolition of all forms of prejudice. It is, at first glance, a very attractive, very sensible religion.

But what do Baha'is believe? What are the origins of their religion? Is their founder, Baha'u'llah, really a prophet of God like

Jesus? What does he say about Jesus? What does he want his followers to do? What is his plan for the world? How do Baha'i teachings compare with those of the Bible?

Origins of the Baha'i Faith

The Baha'i Faith developed in the nineteenth century in Iran, then known as Persia. It is named after its prophet, Baha'u'llah, whose title in Arabic means "Glory of God." Like most Iranians for the past 1,300 years, its founders and early converts were all Shi'ite Muslims.[1]

Of the twelve men Shi'ites recognize as legitimate successors to Muhammad, the last was Imam Mahdi. A recluse, Imam Mahdi communicated with his followers through spokesmen called *Babs* ("Gates"). Ever since communication from him ceased in A.D. 941, devout Shi'ites have awaited his return as a conquering messiah.

In 1844 a twenty-four-year-old Persian wool merchant took the title *Bab* and began to preach a new religion. The Bab claimed to be a prophet greater than Muhammad, sent by God to replace Muhammad's religion and laws with his own. Believers flocked to him. Muslim leaders who did not accept his claims soon locked him in jail, where he spent most of his six-year ministry.

The Bab's followers, called *Babis,* staged several insurrections, mainly in 1848-50.[2] The Persian government suppressed the Babi uprisings with unbridled cruelty. Finally, in an effort to kill the movement at its source, they executed the Bab in 1850.

After his death the Babi community turned for spiritual leadership to twenty-year-old Subh-i-Ezel, whom the Bab had named as his successor.[3] Subh-i-Ezel was poorly suited for leadership, so practical administrative responsibilities fell to his older half-brother, Baha'u'llah. The Babis were harshly persecuted, and their two leaders were banished from Persia to Baghdad, from there to Turkey and then to Bulgaria.

The Bab had taught that a prophet even greater than himself would one day appear. In 1863 Baha'u'llah declared that he was that prophet. Most Babis accepted Baha'u'llah's claim and shifted their devotion from the Bab to him. They became known as Baha'is. The rest, unable to reconcile Baha'u'llah's claim with the Bab's appointment of Subh-i-Ezel as his successor, remained loyal to Subh-i-Ezel. The two factions clashed violently. Believers on both sides were murdered. Subh-i-Ezel and Baha'u'llah each accused the other of attempted poisoning. Finally, in 1868, the civil authorities intervened. They sent Subh-i-Ezel to a prison on Cyprus and Baha'u'llah to a prison at Akka, now in Israel.[4]

Subh-i-Ezel's imprisonment marked the beginning of the end of his influence and of Babism as such. Baha'u'llah's imprisonment, however, only intensified the zeal of the Baha'is.

Every word Baha'u'llah uttered was scrupulously recorded. He dictated over one hundred books and tablets. His book of laws, the *Kitab-i-Aqdas* ("Most Holy Book"), is considered his "most weighty and sacred" work.[5]

Baha'u'llah's imprisonment at Akka lasted two years, though he remained nominally in custody for a few years longer. He died of a fever in 1892 at the age of seventy-five and was buried in Bahji, outside Akka. Before his death he had commanded Baha'is to face the direction of his tomb when they pray.

Baha'u'llah had appointed his eldest son, Abdu'l-Baha, to succeed him. Though he did not claim to be a Manifestation of God like his father, he did assume sole authority to interpret Baha'u'llah's teachings. He claimed infallibility for his interpretations and gave no individual Baha'i "the right to put forth his own opinion or express his particular conviction."[6]

Abdu'l-Baha was primarily responsible for spreading the Baha'i Faith outside the Middle East. He died in 1921, leaving his Oxford-educated grandson, Shoghi Effendi, as Guardian of the Faith. Shoghi Effendi died in 1957 and, in violation of Baha'i law, left no will.[7] He had no heir and appointed no successor. Six years later the first Baha'i Universal House of Justice was elected. Among Baha'is this nine-person board is held to be infallible and governs Baha'i affairs today from their world headquarters in Haifa, Israel.

Baha'i Teachings

Basic Concepts. Baha'u'llah's word for all humanity was Unity. His goal was to unify all religions, peoples and nations under his own banner. He declared that the world's major religions are not contradictory and competitive, but successively updated versions of the same religion. Judaism, Islam, Buddhism, Christianity, Hinduism—all are true. All of them are of God. All agree in their basic principles. They are separated from one another only by time and by inconsequential details.

According to Baha'i teaching, Adam, Abraham, Moses, Krishna, Buddha, Jesus and Muhammad were each members of a single orderly series. They were all Manifestations of God. Each was a genuine prophet of God—a divine, sinless, infallible being. Each taught God's one true religion in a way his own contemporaries could understand. Each had his own heyday, which Baha'is call his "cycle." So Jesus, for instance, taught God's religion to his contemporaries according to the needs of his own time. After six hundred years, though, the times and human needs had changed, so God sent Muhammad to replace Christianity with a new religion, Islam. By 1844 people had outgrown Islam and were ready for the revelation of the Bab. Then by 1863 people needed Baha'u'llah's revelation.

So God's program for his people is an endless cycle of new religion replacing old. Shoghi Effendi wrote that "the fundamental principle which constitutes the bedrock of Baha'i belief [is] the principle that religious truth is not absolute but relative, that Divine Revelation is orderly, continuous and progressive and not spasmodic or final."[8] So what Jesus taught and what the Bible said about him two thousand years ago were true then, but are not necessarily true anymore.

The bottom line for Baha'is then is that Baha'u'llah is God's appointed prophet for today. All previous religions, true as they were for their own time, are now obsolete and therefore canceled. They have all been replaced by the Baha'i Faith. We must therefore abandon allegiance to anachronisms like Jesus and cleave to Baha'u'llah.

Baha'u'llah's Claims. Baha'is go to great lengths to invest Baha'u'llah with biblical credentials. To that end, the Bible passage they quote most often is John 16:12-13, where Jesus says, "There is still much that I could say to you, but the burden would be too great for you now. However, when he comes who is the Spirit of truth, he will guide you into all the truth." Baha'is read this as a confirmation of their fundamental doctrine that each age needs its own updated revelation from God. It is also regarded as a prophecy of Baha'u'llah, the Spirit of truth come to guide us into all truth.

Baha'u'llah claimed to be not only the Spirit of truth, but also Jesus Christ come again, the Everlasting Father, the Speaker on Sinai, Alpha and Omega, and so on. He claimed to be the fulfillment not only of all Christian prophecies, but of many Jewish, Hindu, Buddhist, Zoroastrian and Muslim prophecies as well.[9] In glory, stature and importance, Baha'u'llah eclipsed Jesus and all other Manifestations. He denied being Almighty God himself, but taught that he, like all other Manifestations, was the only source of divine guidance in his cycle.

Here are a few things Baha'u'llah said about himself and his revelation:

He Who is the Best-Beloved is come! He hath crowned Himself with the glory of God's Revelation. . . . Let all eyes rejoice, and let every ear be gladdened, for now is the time to gaze on His beauty, now is the fit time to hearken to His voice.

But for Him [Baha'u'llah] no Divine Messenger would have been invested with the Robe of Prophethood, nor would any of the sacred Scriptures have been revealed.

By the righteousness of Mine own Self! Great, immeasurably great is this Cause! Mighty, inconceivably mighty is this Day!

That which hath been made manifest in this preëminent, this most exalted Revelation, stands unparalleled in the annals of the past, nor will future ages witness its like.[10]

Baha'i Law. Within Baha'i thought the need for each Manifestation is to bring God's laws up to date, to suit the needs of his particular era. Accordingly, Baha'u'llah wrote laws regulating prayer, fasting, marriage, divorce, inheritance and so on, in painstaking detail. He demanded unblinking obedience: Baha'is "must stray not the breadth of a hair from the 'Law.' "[11] Baha'u'llah commanded that a variety of prayers be recited under specified circumstances, in specified postures, at specified times and subject to specified exemptions. Three times each day, for instance, Baha'is must wash their faces and hands, turn toward Baha'u'llah's tomb and recite an Obligatory Prayer. Each day they are required to perform their ablutions, seat themselves and repeat ninety-five times, "Allah-u-Abha" ("God of highest glory"). They must fast from sunup to sundown nineteen days each March, though under certain conditions they may be excused. Baha'is should marry, but men should take no more than two wives. The man must pay a dowry of 2.4 ounces of gold or silver, though he may demand a refund if he discovers his wife is not a virgin.

Baha'u'llah directed each Baha'i to write a will, dividing his estate into 2,520 shares to be distributed by formula among family members. In practice, this formula division takes place only if a Baha'ː dies intestate.

Other laws tell how to behave as a good Baha'i: study the scriptures; fellowship with others; respond to invitations; study languages; consult physicians when ill; be fair and truthful and courteous, and do not be fanatical, hypocritical or contentious; do not plunge your hand into food; stay out of Iranian bath houses.[12]

By such decrees Baha'u'llah is held to have brought God's law up to date, meeting the human needs of this age and those of the next nine hundred years.

Unity. When Baha'is talk about the unity of mankind, or about one world, or the Kingdom of God, they do not mean a mere mood or ethos of togetherness. They mean an international political empire of which the Baha'i Faith would be the state religion.[13]

Baha'is intend to institute, in Shoghi Effendi's words, a Baha'i world Super-State, a commonwealth in which all the peoples of the world would be subject to a single global authority. All nations would waive their national sovereignty and cede key rights to the

Baha'i world Super-State. Every human on the planet would be subject to the Baha'i world parliament, supreme tribunal and an "International Executive adequate to enforce supreme and unchallengeable authority on every recalcitrant member of the commonwealth."[14]

The Baha'i Universal House of Justice would be the supreme governing body. These nine men would be elected by Baha'is, but would not be responsible to them. As a body they would be infallible. They would rule a world in which strife between nations, races, classes and individuals would be no more. No one would have too much, no one too little. Cooperation, peace and sharing would everywhere be the norm. Baha'is themselves describe their World Order as "utopia."[15]

This utopian ambition is not a sideline to the religion. Shoghi Effendi says, "To dissociate the administrative principles of the Cause from the purely spiritual and humanitarian teachings would be tantamount to a mutilation of the body of the Cause."[16]

Abdu'l-Baha, regarded as infallible, promised that the Baha'i utopia would become reality during the twentieth century: "The unity of nations . . . in this century will be securely established, causing all the peoples of the world to regard themselves as citizens of one common fatherland."[17]

Teachings about Jesus. Baha'i literature circulated in the West is meant to appeal to people with a Christian orientation, so Jesus is mentioned and quoted often. But since the Baha'i Faith developed within the context of Islam, Jesus has in fact never been of more than peripheral importance in the Baha'i outlook.

Baha'is honor him as one of many Manifestations of God whose era of importance has come and gone. His career as Lord ended in A.D. 622 when Muhammad began his ministry. Christ's teachings are not to be rejected, but neither should they be given undue attention. Jesus' status has been successively overshadowed by that of Muhammad, the Bab and Baha'u'llah.

Jesus was not the incarnation of God, but a Manifestation of God. Baha'is liken a Manifestation to a mirror that reflects the sun:

the sun (God) does not descend into the mirror nor is the mirror identical with the sun. "Was Christ within God, or God within Christ? No, in the name of God!"[18]

Christ's death and resurrection are rarely mentioned in Baha'i scripture. His death, like that of any martyr, may be inspirational and encouraging, but bears no unique or eternal significance. Baha'u'llah equated the crucifixion of Christ with the accidental death of his own son, who fell through a skylight onto a wooden crate. Baha'u'llah offered up his "martyred" son "as a 'ransom' for the regeneration of the world and the unification of its peoples."[19]

Christ's resurrection was not a literal, physical event, but a figure of speech. "The resurrections of the Divine Manifestations are not of the body... and have no connection with material things." Abdu'l-Baha tells what really happened: "The disciples were troubled and agitated after the martyrdom of Christ.... The Cause of Christ was like a lifeless body; and, when after three days the disciples became assured and steadfast, ... his religion found life, his teachings and his admonitions became evident and visible."[20]

So to Baha'is the resurrection was not something that happened to the flesh and bones of the Nazarene, but something that happened in the minds of his disciples. When they announced that Jesus had risen from the dead, therefore, all they really meant was that on the third day they had simultaneously overcome their depression.

A Christian Response

Basic Concepts. Baha'i beliefs begin with the concept of Manifestations of God, beings "pure from every sin, and sanctified from faults."[21] According to the Bible, though, the men who head the Baha'i list were ordinary sinners like you and me. Adam disobeyed God and is best remembered for his disobedience. Abraham, on at least two occasions, bought his own safety at the expense of innocent men, who suffered gravely by falling for his selfish, premeditated deception (Gen 12:10-20; 20:1-18). Moses, by his own admission, murdered an Egyptian, hid the body and fled (Ex 2:11-15). God denied him entry into the Promised Land for one reason: his disobedience of a direct command of God (Num 20; Deut 32:48-52).

As essential as Adam, Abraham and Moses are in the structure of Baha'i theology, they nevertheless each fall short of the status Baha'is ascribe to them.

Moreover, while most of the Manifestations taught one God, Krishna taught many gods and Gautama Buddha taught no god. Such differences are too fundamental to permit acceptance of Baha'u'llah's premise that they were all "uttering the same speech, and proclaiming the same Faith."[22]

The Baha'i appeal to "the needs of the times" is based on several dubious assumptions. It assumes that all people progress uniformly in the development of their spiritual, intellectual and moral capacities. It assumes that the typical person of any one century is necessarily more sophisticated spiritually and intellectually than the typical person of any previous century. We usually think of human progress in terms of scientific and technological advances, and in that sense progress is obvious, though not uniform. But the domain of religion is moral, ethical and spiritual affairs. Here differences between centuries become obscure. The two fundamental questions Baha'is must answer, therefore, are (1) How does the person on the street in the twentieth century differ *morally* from the typical person of any previous century? and (2) How does the Baha'i Faith satisfy the particular needs of this century in a way that no other religion can?

I have heard no convincing answer to the first question. Nor have I seen any evidence that we today are any less likely to lie, steal, cheat or otherwise sin than were people five hundred or five thousand years ago. Nor are we any more likely to heed the holy men.

The second question, how the Baha'i Faith alone suits the particular needs of today, takes us to the heart of the religion. Baha'u'llah argues strongly that old religion will not do in a new age, that people today need a religion for today. But he does not deliver what he promises. There is little about the Baha'i Faith to commend it expressly to the twentieth century. The laws of the *Kitab-i-Aqdas* have little in particular to do with the twentieth century. For the most part they would suit the eighth century B.C. or the twenty-fourth century A.D. equally well. Baha'is say the promise of Unity, of a Baha'i world Super-State, is what suits the needs of these times. But telling us what we need and providing it are two very different things. Dr. John Esslemont personally heard Abdu'l-Baha pinpoint the year by which "universal Peace will be firmly established, ... [and] misunderstandings will pass away." The year he predicted was 1957.[23]

The Baha'i appeal to the needs of the times is also contradicted by the Faith's own history. Although twelve hundred years passed between Muhammad and the Bab, only thirteen years separated the Bab's ministry from Baha'u'llah's. How had human needs changed between 1850 and 1863? Hardly anyone outside of Persia had even *heard* of the Bab before Baha'u'llah supplanted his revelation with a new one. Had people's moral character changed so radically between 1850 and 1863 that the Bab's religion no longer suited the needs of the times, if indeed it ever did? Baha'u'llah did not want to discuss such questions. "That so brief an interval" should have separated himself from the Bab, he wrote, "is a secret that no man can unravel, and a mystery such as no mind can fathom. Its duration had been foreordained."[24]

Baha'u'llah's Claims. Even if one were to accept in theory the Baha'i argument that the present era requires a new prophet of God, it would not necessarily follow that Baha'u'llah is the one. He must prove himself.

Of the many Bible prophecies Baha'u'llah claims to fulfill, none is cited by Baha'is more often than Christ's promise of the Spirit of truth in John 14—16.

The first time Jesus mentions the Spirit of truth, he calls him "your Advocate, ... the Spirit of truth." The second time, Jesus calls him "your Advocate, the Holy Spirit" (Jn 14:16-17, 26). "Spirit of truth" and "Holy Spirit" are two names for the same Spirit. Jesus said nearly two thousand years ago that his promise of the Holy Spirit of truth would be fulfilled "within the next few days" (Acts 1:5), and it was. The fulfillment at Pentecost is recorded in Acts 2.

Nevertheless, Baha'is portray the Spirit of truth as a messianic figure, Christ's successor, who was awaited vainly by the apostles. Baha'u'llah claims that his own ministry constitutes the coming of the Spirit of truth. Let us look at Baha'u'llah's claims closely in comparison with a few important things Jesus said about the Spirit of truth.

First, Jesus said that the Spirit of truth "will teach you everything, and will call to mind all that I have told you" (Jn 14:26). The Spirit of truth, according to Jesus, would confirm and explain his teaching, not replace it. The Baha'i concept of a Manifestation of God is quite different. A Manifestation, which Baha'u'llah claims to be, overrules and supplants the teachings of earlier prophets. While borrowing Jesus' phrase, Baha'u'llah claims authority to do the opposite of what Jesus said the Spirit of truth would do.

Jesus said the Spirit of truth "will be with you for ever . . . dwells with you and is in you" (Jn 14:16-17). Baha'u'llah lived with us for seventy-five years but died in 1892. Baha'is do not claim that he ever rose from the dead in any sense, so he is certainly no longer with us physically. Nor do Baha'is claim that he maintains any kind of spiritual intercourse with his people today: believers study his teachings and learn spiritual things from them, but in no sense is Baha'u'llah still with or in them, as Jesus said the Spirit of truth would be.

Abdu'l-Baha quotes Jesus' saying, "Whatever he shall hear, that shall he speak" (Jn 16:13), and concludes, "It is therefore clear that the Spirit of Truth is embodied in a man who has individuality, who has ears to hear and a tongue to speak."[25] Besides being inconsistent with his own rigorous rejection of anthropomorphism, Abdu'l-Baha's interpretation conflicts with Jesus' statement that the Spirit of truth is not someone or something that can be seen (Jn 14:17).

Jesus also said the Spirit of truth would glorify him (Jn 16:14). Far from glorifying Jesus, Baha'u'llah belittled him by equating his death ("by the deliberate will and plan of God"—Acts 2:23) with the accidental death of one of Baha'u'llah's own children.

In sum, Jesus' promise of the Spirit of truth was fulfilled when the Holy Spirit came at Pentecost nearly two thousand years ago. Baha'u'llah failed to do the things Jesus said the Spirit would do. He can draw support from Jesus only by ignoring what he actually said about the Spirit of truth.

Baha'i Law. Baha'u'llah intended his laws to stand as the basis of civilization for a thousand years. Many of them are fine, timeless principles, which any Baha'i, Christian or atheist could welcome and practice. But the Baha'i position is that they are above all timely, that they suit the needs of this particular age.

One need only read the laws, however, to realize that they are not intrinsically applicable to today, much less to the future. What is unique about this era in history that necessitates, for instance, burial in stone or hardwood coffins? In what way do this and previous generations differ, that only now are we prohibited from having congregational prayer? If we today can benefit by repeating "Allah-u-Abha" ninety-five times a day, how were people different two thousand years ago that they could not have so benefited?

In practice, Baha'is consider few of Baha'u'llah's laws currently binding. They say we are not yet ready for them. That only weakens their argument that his new religion alone suits the needs of this age. It also conficts with Baha'u'llah's own demand that his people not only recognize him but also "observe every ordinance of Him Who is the Desire of the world [i.e., Baha'u'llah]. These twin duties are inseparable. Neither is acceptable without the other."[26]

Some of Baha'u'llah's laws have been effectively eliminated by official interpretation. For instance, though Baha'u'llah permits bigamy, his son Abdu'l-Baha ruled that "bigamy is conditioned upon justice, and as justice is impossible, it follows that bigamy is not permissible, and monogamy alone should be practised."[27]

He eliminated Baha'u'llah's unwieldy inheritance laws in a similar way.

Not only have many laws been postponed and others eliminated, but the book containing Baha'u'llah's laws, the *Kitab-i-Aqdas,* is not generally available today. Portions of it have been translated into English, but Baha'is say we are not yet ready for the rest. This is a remarkable argument, considering that the *Aqdas* was one of Baha'u'llah's most widely read books during his lifetime. It is also difficult to understand why, when a Christian scholar published an English translation of the *Aqdas,* Baha'is were forbidden by their leaders to read it.[28]

A Christian's problem with the Baha'i concept of law goes far beyond the availability or relevance of individual laws. A Christian must question the fundamental Baha'i concept that, while everything else changes over the centuries, the one thing that does not change is the pattern of new religion replacing old. According to the Bible, God's revelation through Jesus is not subject to replacement by any newer, higher or more complete revelation. Christ's was not merely the most complete revelation up to his time (as Baha'is are taught), but God's ultimate revelation for all time. God sent prophet after prophet for centuries, but the coming of Jesus represents something altogether different and unprecedented, a whole new policy: "When in former times God spoke to our forefathers, he spoke in fragmentary and varied fashion through the prophets. But in this the final age he has spoken to us in the Son" (Heb 1:1-2). Having "appeared once and for all at the climax of history," Jesus' dominion "is for ever and ever. . . . The heavens . . . shall pass away, but thou [the Son] endurest; . . . they shall be changed like any garment. But thou art the same, and thy years shall have no end" (Heb 9:26; 1:8, 10-12).

The Baha'i theory that God sends new prophets to replace the obsolete religion and laws of old prophets breaks down when we come to Jesus. His law, love, can never grow old and therefore need never be replaced. Baha'u'llah himself admits as much: "Know thou that in every age and dispensation all divine ordinances are changed and transformed according to the requirement of the time, except the law of love, which, like a fountain, always flows and is never overtaken by change."[29]

Unity. The Baha'i Faith teaches the unity of all humankind. So does the Bible. Baha'is plan to institutionalize that unity in a global Baha'i empire. The Bible offers no such program. But it does teach that, at the right time, all creation will be brought into a holy unity. The question, then, is, Around whom will all be unified? Who will be king in the kingdom?

Shoghi Effendi says that Baha'u'llah will be "enthroned in the hearts and consciences of the masses, . . . His undisputed ascendency . . . universally recognized." With the Baha'i Faith as their state religion, people will have reached "that golden millennium —the Day when the kingdoms of this world shall have become the Kingdom of God Himself, the Kingdom of Baha'u'llah."[30]

Christians will recognize that last statement as a perversion of Revelation 11:15 (KJV): "The kingdoms of this world are become the kingdoms of our Lord, and of his Christ." Whenever the Bible touches on unity, it always places Jesus himself as the agent of that unity. He is king in the kingdom:

[God] has made known to us his hidden purpose—such was his will and pleasure determined beforehand in Christ—to be put into effect when the time was ripe: namely, that the universe, all in heaven and on earth, might be brought into a unity in Christ. (Eph 1:9-10)

There is no such thing as Jew and Greek, slave and freeman, male and female; for you are all one person in Christ Jesus. (Gal 3:28)

Through him [Jesus] God chose to reconcile the whole universe to himself, making peace through the shedding of his blood upon the cross—to reconcile all things, whether on earth or in heaven, through him alone. (Col 1:20)

It will not do to imagine that when these passages say Jesus Christ they really mean the Manifestation and therefore Baha'u'llah. In context they refer clearly to the unique Son of God who was incarnate once for all in Jesus of Nazareth.

Teachings about Jesus. What Baha'is are taught about Jesus is not so much untrue as inadequate. Jesus was a Manifestation of God in the Baha'i sense, but he was infinitely more than that. Baha'is draw some meaning from his death and resurrection but fail to come to grips with their implications.

The Bible says two things so often and so plainly that we all must face them. The first is that our sin separates us from God and renders us "dead in our sins" (Eph 2:5). The second is that Christ's death and resurrection stand as the sole basis for forgiving our sin, bringing us to life spiritually and reconciling us to God (Rom 5:6-11).

These matters have been of little interest to Baha'is. More important to them have been recognizing Baha'u'llah as God's new prophet, following his teachings and ordinances, loving God, fellowshiping with the Baha'i community and doing one's part to bring about the Baha'i world Super-State. In the process one attains "perfections" and makes progress toward God. By praying, doing good works and having others do the same on one's behalf, one may persuade God to forgive sins. Jesus' dying for one's sins does not enter into Baha'i thinking.

The Baha'i approach fails to answer the fundamental question: Why should God forgive our sins? The implied answer is that he forgives because he is gracious. But grace and love are very small aspects of the portrait Baha'u'llah paints of God. Baha'is look to God's justice. Abdu'l-Baha says, "The canopy of existence resteth upon the pole of justice, and not of forgiveness."[31] But unmitigated justice is the last thing a sinner wants from God. His justice can leave him no choice but to condemn us. Only his grace, expressed in Christ, can offer us hope for forgiveness.

The Baha'i approach is basically a matter of trying to merit God's favor. But God unequivocally rejects our righteous deeds—what Baha'is would call perfections—as filthy rags in his sight (Is 64:6). The Baha'i approach would have us stop turning our backs on God and start trying to move toward him—which is fine—but overlooks the barrier of sin blocking our path. Our sin has to be dealt with in some radical way because it renders us spiritually dead. Unless and until something radical is done about our sin, it is pointless to try to serve God, please him or get closer to him.

Because we are spiritually dead in sin, we must be born again. We can be born again only by being identified with Christ in his resurrection (1 Pet 1:3; Eph 2:4-7). That process of identifying with Jesus requires an undivided allegiance to Jesus as unique Lord of our life.

The meaning and significance of Christ's death is central to Christian teaching. Without the crucifixion, Christianity would be just another toothless religion telling us to believe in God and behave ourselves. But on the cross Jesus accomplished something unique in all history. He dissolved the sin barrier separating us from God by taking on himself the penalty we deserve. That's radical. God invites us now to be reconciled to him by accepting what Jesus has done on our behalf and giving our allegiance to him. He is the only one whose efforts on our behalf are recognized by God (1 Tim 2:5; Acts 4:12). Other religious teachers may well alter God's standing in our sight; only Jesus can alter our standing in God's sight.

But Jesus has done more than die for our sins. He has also risen from the dead. The Bible teaches that Jesus literally awakened from physical death.[32] Everything else in the New Testament depends on that for its meaning. Paul stresses the importance of the resurrection in this way: "If Christ was not raised, then our gospel is null and void, and so is your faith; and we turn out to be lying witnesses for God" (1 Cor 15:14-15).

The unique beauty of Christianity is that we do not serve the memory of a dead holy man. Because he rose, Jesus is alive. He is Lord, right now, today. He has not abdicated in favor of Muhammad or Baha'u'llah. "His reign shall never end" (Lk 1:33). His is "an everlasting sovereignty which should not pass away, and his kingly power such as should never be impaired" (Dan 7:14).

Baha'u'llah offers a religious system; Jesus offers new life in relationship with God. Baha'u'llah offers rules and regulations to tell you how to live your life; Jesus offers to live his life in and through you. Baha'u'llah offers to take Christ's place and give us new teachings; Jesus has not given up his place and continues to offer eternal truth.

You can give your allegiance to Baha'u'llah or to Jesus. But don't imagine you can give it to both. Lordship is something Jesus does not share. "This is why Christ died and came to life again, to establish his lordship over dead and living" (Rom 14:9).[33]

The good news Christians have to share is that "the priesthood which Jesus holds is perpetual, because he remains for ever. That is why he is able to save absolutely those who approach God through him; he is always living to plead on their behalf" (Heb 7:24-25).

Pronunciation Guide
Abdu'l-Baha—AB-dool bah-HAH
Bab—BOB
Babi—BOB-ee
Baha'i—Bah-HIGH or bah-HAH-ee
Baha'u'llah—bah-HAH-oo-lah
Shi'ite—SHEE-ite
Shoghi Effendi—SHOW-ghee e-FEN-dee

3

Bhagwan Shree Rajneesh

Eckart Floether
with Eric Pement

*Nobody is a sinner.... I tell you, there is
no need for salvation, it is within you.*
Bhagwan Shree Rajneesh

I JUST DON'T WANT ANYBODY TO tell me what to do!" Jim, a family man and a successful architect from South Dakota, is blowing off steam about his boss and the demands and pressures of work. Tired of social duplicity, he is planning to spend another weekend dancing and chanting in a California meditation center. The center is sponsored by one of America's newest spiritual movements, one headed by the Indian guru Bhagwan Shree Rajneesh.

When he is among the guru's devotees, Jim is lavished with attention. He finds the comfort and compassion of the communal atmosphere inviting. Orange-clad followers with symbolic wooden necklaces listen to his problems and psychically perceive unspoken injuries suffered during his childhood. At the center, Jim experiences altered states of consciousness through meditation and sees psychedelic visions similar to those experienced under the influence of hallucinogenic drugs.

After these experiences, Jim seems markedly different. His office colleagues say he looks "spaced-out," and he talks more about enlightenment than about the construction business. They place a number of calls across the country, looking for help.

Who is Bhagwan Shree Rajneesh, and what is his movement all about?

The Man Rajneesh

According to an officially approved biography, Rajneesh was born "the eldest in a family of five sisters and seven brothers in a small village in central India on the 11th December 1931" as Rajneesh Chandra Mohan.[1]

His father was an unsuccessful businessman who did not belong to the highest Indian caste. Rajneesh spent much of his early childhood with his grandparents. A major crisis occurred when he witnessed his grandfather's illness and gradual death. The seven-year-old boy had been deeply attached to the old man, and this event changed his life overnight.[2]

Rajneesh became increasingly preoccupied with death. He would follow funeral processions as eagerly as other children might follow a circus, and he often spent the night in a cremation ground near his home. At the age of fourteen, he entered a ruined temple, lay down, and waited several days for death to overtake him.

In college, Rajneesh studied philosophy and psychology and gained some background in photography, debate and painting. He also served as assistant editor for a daily paper. He claims that during his college days, at the age of twenty-one, he became "enlightened." Rajneesh eventually earned an M.A. in philosophy from Saugur University in 1957.

From 1957 to 1966 he taught philosophy in two colleges. Feeling compelled to awaken humanity from its spiritual lethargy, he also traveled throughout India "giving outrageously abrasive and controversial talks" on politics, religion and sexual attitudes.[3]

In 1964 he gave his first course in meditation at a ten-day retreat in Rajasthan. His reputation as a spiritual rebel grew rapidly. He quit his post at the University of Jabalpur in August 1966 to devote more time to his speaking career and meditation retreats. His brilliant intellect and vast knowledge of India's history and philosophy suited him well for public speaking. Understandably many were drawn to him.

However, constant instruction in what he called "the ABC's of enlightenment" to an ever-changing stream of new faces displeased him, for Rajneesh had no opportunity to teach a single group the "XYZ's." Therefore, in 1969 he stopped traveling and settled down in Bombay with a small group of his disciples. This group later formed the nucleus of the community which he began in Poona, India, an industrial city a hundred twenty miles southeast of Bombay. There Rajneesh took on the name *Bhagwan* (God) and in 1974 organized an *ashram* (a religious settlement or retreat) to implement his vision. His middle name, *Shree,* translates as "sir."

Most disciples coming to Poona (many from Western nations) attempted to live in Rajneesh's presence for as long as possible. At the ashram, the devotees received personal instruction from Rajneesh or ashram personnel as to what they should do: move onto the grounds, live in Poona for a while, or return to their native countries. Those who were lucky enough to be chosen to stay in the ashram were told how to conduct every area of their lives. This included what type of work to do (without getting paid), whether to start or end a relationship, what courses to take, what work and sex partners to have, and whether to abort or carry a child.

While the ashram itself contained only about three hundred residents, up to seven or eight thousand Western devotees lived outside the ashram, in or near Poona. And the commune received perhaps seven thousand visitors each day. The cost of living in Poona was not very high, yet since every available job was taken, many Westerners wound up either dealing drugs or in prostitution to support themselves.

For those who dwelt within the ashram's walls, the strong bonds between master and disciple were deepened in that the ashram supplied the disciple's biological needs as well as emotional and religious ones. The one and only commitment required of the devotee was complete surrender to Rajneesh and unquestioning acceptance of his word.

Rajneesh's Mission

Rajneesh has voiced much concern and criticism about the sickness of our world. In 1979 he warned: "If we cannot create the 'new man' in the coming twenty years, then humanity has no future. The holocaust of a global suicide can be avoided only if a new kind of man can be created."[4]

Rajneesh sees himself on the vanguard of the New Consciousness. He explains, "Buddhahood [enlightenment] has existed, but nobody has ever tried to research the awakened mind, to create a scientific discipline out of it. It has always been an individual phenomenon."[5] Presently, becoming a Buddha or becoming enlightened "happens so suddenly that there is no space to study it"; thus Rajneesh proposes to study this process of enlightenment.

Toward this end, the ashram provides not only a place of instruction and meditation, but a place where Rajneesh can experiment with new meditation techniques, creating a *Buddhafield* for his devotees. "Buddhafield means a situation where your sleeping Buddha can be awakened. Buddhafield means an energyfield where you can start your journey, maturing, where your sleep can be broken," a place "where you can be shocked into awareness."[6] Carrying out these experimentations, Rajneesh has devised his own unique brand of meditation, specially made for nervous and time-conscious Western peoples.

Rajneesh is convinced his mission to bring enlightenment to humanity is the fulfillment of a task he began seven centuries ago. He relates that in his previous life, as a one-hundred-six-year-old *bodhisattva* (a Buddha-to-be) with thousands of disciples, he was on the verge of achieving final enlightenment and so forever leaving the body. But for his followers' sake, he arranged his own murder three days short of enlightment, in order that he might have the opportunity to aid them in a future reincarnation.

Seven hundred years later he came back as Rajneesh and achieved complete enlightenment at a young age because of his great advancement in that earlier life. Rajneesh has told many of his devotees that they followed him in a previous life. His mission is to gather his followers together, enabling them to attain enlightenment as he has.

After seven years, the Shree Rajneesh ashram in Poona was attracting thousands each day. Seemingly at the height of his popularity, Rajneesh entered what he calls "the ultimate stage of my work." In March 1981 he stopped talking. The arrival of this phase, called "the Silence," had been announced to his disciples as early as 1977, but its coming threw many into shock. After years of lecturing, Rajneesh felt that only through silence could he communicate his ultimate message. (He now speaks only to his physician and a few of his closest aides.)

Within a few weeks, Rajneesh applied for a tourist visa to the United States and, taking a Pan Am flight, arrived in New York on June 1, 1981. He was followed by thirteen tons of personal luggage. His flock was left behind in utter bewilderment and despair, and piece by piece the ashram was dissolved.

In August the news broke that his American disciples had purchased over 100 square miles of ranch land near Antelope, Oregon, for $6 million and were leasing another 17,000 acres. It gradually became evident that the group was planning to build a new ashram to replace the one in India. A Rajneesh newsletter dated September 1981 said the project "is going to be the beginning of a new humanity."[7]

The devotees have named the property *Rajneeshpuram* ("expression of Rajneesh") and made arrangements to legally incorporate three and a half square miles of the ranch as a city. Many of them envision a self-sufficient community for half a million people with its own government, hospitals, schools, stores and law enforcement agency.

Soon after the new property was acquired, Bhagwan Shree Rajneesh moved into it and was furnished with his own house, library, numerous Rolls Royces and a twin-engine airplane. Rajneesh recently applied to the U.S. Department of Immigration for permanent resident status as a "religious teacher."

Rajneesh's Movement

Rajneesh considers himself to be the "Master of the masters" and therefore cannot instruct just anybody. He deals only with those who are at the end of their journey and on the brink of enlightenment. To Rajneesh, "only the rich can become spiritual," for the poor are still fighting to survive and are enthralled with a worldly career.[8] As a result, Rajneesh has attracted a following of sharp people from the Western world, many from upper-income brackets.

Initiation. It is considered something very special to be an initiated member in the movement. A full-fledged devotee is called a *sannyasin* and can be recognized by the orange or red clothing worn both at home and at work. (*Sannyasin* is Sanskrit for "one who is under a vow of renunciation.")

The ritual of initiation is a very powerful experience for almost all who undergo it, and the event is often spoken of as a spiritual rebirth. In the ceremony, Rajneesh gives his kneeling disciple a *mala* (a necklace of wooden beads with a locket displaying Rajneesh's photograph), which is worn with the orange clothing as a sign of discipleship. Then he presses the initiate's forehead with his thumb and "opens his third eye," an experience that often elicits a strong physical response, said to be "cosmic energy." Finally, the devotee is given a piece of paper, signed by Rajneesh, with a selected Hindu name, which severs him or her from all past identity. Should this blissful sensation fade away, and it does, the disciple is free to ask for another energy filling from the Master. Such "recharges" normally take place every six months.

Enlightenment. Rajneesh is not just a humanistic psychologist.

His meditation centers provide consciousness-altering techniques ranging from the martial arts to mirror-gazing, from the saturation experience of "rebirthing" to Lilly sensory-deprivation tanks, and from free sex to Zen Buddhism.

To obtain the ultimate experience that Rajneesh offers, devotees must trust him implicitly and be willing to meet whatever demands Rajneesh makes. They must be ready to give up not only their families and occupations, but their minds and personalities, to become "passive" and "mindless."[9] Rajneesh asserts, "Mind is a prison."[10] To reach ultimate truth, devotees must also abandon their previous God(s): "All your worship is sheer stupidity."[11] "You don't know where God is. He has never given his address to anybody, ever." But, Rajneesh adds, "a guru is the address of God."[12] Rajneesh leaves no doubt that God's address corresponds with his own.

The Rajneesh ashram in Poona was characterized by the acceptance of violence and sex in its therapy. Rajneesh and his group leaders believe that the beauty, uniqueness and divine nature of man can emerge only when suppressed emotional patterns and sensual desires are acted out.

Until March of 1979, violent outbursts of uncontrollable rage, profanity and physical aggression took place in Rajneesh's encounter groups around the world. Hospitals in Poona were called upon to treat the broken bones of sannyasins who were attacked by fellow devotees working out their suppressed anger. German filmmaker Wolfgang Dobrowolny, a former sannyasin himself, filmed the well-publicized documentary *Ashram*, which contains actual footage of beatings, bones being broken, and an attempted rape during a therapy session. The Rajneesh Foundation in 1979 issued orders disallowing physical violence in its workshops, although verbal expressions of pent-up anger were still being encouraged by group leaders after their rejection of violence.

Up to 1979, sexual encounters were also frequent and were considered an important stage of spiritual growth. Two female disciples told me they had themselves sterilized because they wanted to preserve all their energy for their personal growth.

In July of 1979, in a group called *Samarpan*, I witnessed an English-born group leader having sexual intercourse in the presence of the group with a sannyasin who was mourning the death of her parents. His comment to her was, "All you need is sex." During the same month, I saw two men in the group have sexual relations with a woman. In my opinion, she did not participate voluntarily. The group leader did not intervene, saying, "It certainly had a therapeutic effect on her."

In my opinion, what really happened in Rajneesh's ashram was not the breaking down of emotional barriers and unnecessary psychological blocks, but unskilled experimentation with human lives and mental states. The so-called liberation of the person was often accompanied by the disintegration of the personality. The local mental hospital in Poona still carries evidence of some of the damage done to sannyasins in therapies and workshops. Several spiritual seekers had to be admitted to this hospital prior to being sent back to their home countries. In Bombay, the West German consulate alone handled fifty to sixty such cases each year.

The numerous techniques Rajneesh employs seem to be designed to produce a loss of personal identity, and the methods are apparently quite effective. A number of people (including professors, lawyers, architects and teachers) have been found wandering the streets, totally disoriented. They did not know who they were, where they were, or what they wanted. The reason Rajneesh wishes to induce such experiences can be understood by looking at his philosophy.

Rajneesh's Teachings

Trying to understand Rajneesh can be a confusing, frustrating experience. His entire aim is to overthrow one's reliance on the mind, so he sees nothing wrong with contradicting himself or giving two people different answers to the same question. However, when a large number of Rajneesh's messages are examined at length, a recognizable ideology emerges.

Authority. It would not be out of order to ask, How can one know whether or not Rajneesh's message is true? To begin with, Rajneesh forbids the use of the mind to determine the truth of his claims. If we are to experience God, he argues, the human mind cannot be involved in the process, for it causes us to see a hostile, divided universe. "We never think that the death of the mind will be a freedom for us," he says.[13] But he insists it is.

Since the mind cannot make definitive statements about ultimate truth, if Rajneesh's claims are to be confirmed at all, it must be through personal, mystical experience. Rajneesh feels his teachings cannot be communicated, only experienced. Therefore words can neither evaluate nor criticize his teachings.

Often, acceptance of Rajneesh as a guru depends as much on sheer surrender as it does on mystical experience. Rajneesh has frequently insisted on this point: "From the one who is being initiated, nothing but surrender will do. Initiation means to be surrendered. . . . It can never be partial. If you surrender partially, you are not surrendering."[14] Indeed, Rajneesh feels no need to provide anyone with rationale for his claims. To question at all is taken as a sign of unenlightenment, resistance and spiritual dullness.

Rajneesh's authority rests solely upon his own assertion, and the devotee has no choice but to drop all questioning and to surrender totally. There is no higher court of appeal.

God. God and the universe are not two separate things, as Rajneesh views them. He has often warned, "When you think in terms of duality, God becomes a false God. There is no God sitting somewhere, presiding over the world. The very world, the very being is God. God is not a person, but a process."[15]

Rajneesh rejects the distinction between the Creator and the creation because he is a monist; that is, he believes that all of reality is made up of a single quality or essence. Sometimes Rajneesh calls it God, while at other times he calls it Silence, Void, Brahman, Beingness or Consciousness. Whatever apparent differences may exist in this ineffable reality, they are only illusory, as everything is made out of the same stuff—consciousness. Thus everything can be called God, and "all that exists is divine. Existence is divine; to exist is to be divine."[16]

The premise that nothing exists but God forces Rajneesh to deny even his own existence and that of his listeners: "The person is nonexistent, a nonentity.... As far as I am concerned, I do not feel that I am a person at all.... And when I refer to 'me,' there is no one who is being referred to. It is only a linguistic device in order for you to understand what I am saying. In fact, there is no one who can be referred to as 'me' or 'you,' but then language will be impossible."[17]

Humanity. Rajneesh teaches that the mind of man prevents him from seeing the oneness of all things. It divides up reality, creating artificial dichotomies, placing us "here" and God "there." But this, says Rajneesh, is faulty understanding. Rajneesh believes that man does not realize that he is truth (or God) because he is unenlightened and ignorant. We are ignorant because we try to know reality by our intellect.[18]

Another problem with man is the *ego*, which man mistakenly believes to be his true self. Man's true self is God, understood as emptiness or void; and man's false self is the ego or mind, causing the illusion of individuality. Rajneesh declares, "The self is not something to be protected; it is something to be destroyed."[19]

Man's struggle is with the ego, which is always active, always thinking; it desires purpose, meaning, fulfillment and survival of the self. Rajneesh argues, however, that existence is nonpurposive —it is play.[20] Thus, it is necessary to "drop" or abandon the ego.

Deliverance. Rajneesh maintains that, in the absolute sense, humanity needs no deliverance and no salvation. "Nobody is a sinner. Even while you are in the darkest hole of your life, you are still divine. You cannot lose your divinity. I tell you, there is no need for salvation, it is within you."[21]

However, man is not "awakened" to his inner bliss and perfection, so he needlessly lives in misery and fear. Rajneesh promises that these negative experiences will vanish and enlightenment will occur when we realize there is no duality of God and non-God.

Rajneesh leans heavily on the doctrine of the void: the more nearly we are passive and empty, the more closely we approximate God. The purpose of his meditations, workshops, lectures, therapies and even sex groups is to bring about this state of emptiness, creating the mindless man. The mindless man is the enlightened man: he has no past, no future, no thought, no attachment, no mind, no ego, no self.

The way of deliverance is broad in theory, but in practice Rajneesh keeps it quite narrow. Rajneesh will say that many paths are possible in which the seeker may become awakened. But he notes many times that the masters who created those paths are now dead, and, for most people, enlightenment is possible only in the presence of a living master. For those who seek enlightenment today, he points to himself. In an unabashed theft from the words of Christ, Rajneesh once remarked: "To them [my followers] I can say: I am a Master. To them I can say: Come to me and drink out of me, and you will not be thirsty, ever."[22]

A Christian Response

Authority. For the Christian, the mere fact that Rajneesh claims enlightenment is not sufficient reason for us to lay down our all and follow him. There are thousands who claim religious authority on the basis of their private mystical experiences. They cannot all be correct.

Neither can the fact that Rajneesh brings about altered states of consciousness in his followers be considered verification of his claims. The fact that he can do so only proves that a transcendent experience is reproducible in others; it does not mean that contact is being made with the Ultimate (that is, God), or that altered states are qualitatively higher, truer or more valid than normal states of consciousness.

The Christian faith cites the Bible as its authority for matters of faith and practice. I do not have the space to discuss in depth the superiority of the biblical revelation over the mystical subjectivism of Rajneesh and other Eastern teachers. Suffice it to say that Scripture is authenticated in part by "the majesty of its themes, by the unity of its message, and by the power of its influence."[23] The authority of Scripture has been a doctrine accepted by the Christian church for eighteen centuries. Scripture does not contradict itself (unlike Rajneesh), and different parts of Scripture attest to the authority of the whole of Scripture (see for example 2 Tim 3:16; 2 Pet 1:19-21). (Readers who wish to investigate this topic further are encouraged to see the reading list on page 214.) From Scripture we learn certain things about God and humanity.

God. Rajneesh's entire philosophy must either stand or fall on the validity of monism. The Bible presents a God very different from Rajneesh's constantly evolving Beingness, a God little more than a synonym for emptiness. Scripture declares from the very beginning that God is the Creator of the universe. "In the beginning God created the heavens and the earth" (Gen 1:1). "I am the LORD, who made all things,/who stretched out the heavens alone,/ who spread out the earth—Who was with me?" (Is 44:24).

In these passages, God is seen not only as Creator, but as possessing self-identity and personality. God speaks using the personal pronoun *I*, and distinguishes himself from the beings he is speaking to. The Bible portrays God as being both immanent to the world and transcendent (see Deut 4:39; Ps 139:3-12; Is 66:1; Jer 23:23-24; Acts 17:27-28). We must not confuse God's immanence (his nearness, approachability) with pantheism, which actually identifies the universe *with* God.

I am the LORD, and there is no other,
> besides me there is no God; . . .

I made the earth,
> and created man upon it;

it was my hands that stretched out the heavens,
> and I commanded all their host. (Is 45:5, 12)

The Bible affirms God's transcendence. Although God is in the world, he is separate and distinct from it. Once it has been established that there is a personal and transcendent Creator-God, then monism is impossible and every other area of Rajneesh's philosophy is radically affected.

In addition to being immanent and transcendent, God is holy and perfect (Lev 11:44; Josh 24:19; Is 57:15). He cannot tolerate imperfection or injustice.

Humanity. Christianity asserts that in contrast to the holiness of God, humanity is imperfect. "All have sinned and fall short of the glory of God," says Paul in Romans 3:23. Sin is a violation of God's moral standards. All of us have failed in our duties to God and to our fellow man, and the Scripture is quite clear that sin is universal: "If we say we have no sin, we deceive ourselves, and the truth is not in us" (1 Jn 1:8).

By contrast, Rajneesh's denial of sin is one of the pillars of his teaching. "I declare that you are not sinners, that no one is a sinner," he announces. "I declare that God resides in you in his utter purity. You are virgin Gods."[24] Rajneesh denies both sin and guilt. For Rajneesh, man's problem is one of ignorance—not recognizing his inner divine perfection. It is worthwhile to observe that if Rajneesh is right and man is innately divine, then the divine is self-deceived (thinking itself imperfect) and thus is innately flawed.

According to the Bible, the human problem is one of rebellion— not admitting innate sinfulness. Not only does man's fallen nature prevent him from becoming what he can be and from fulfilling the purpose for which God designed him, but his fallenness also incurs the judgment of God. In a very judicial sense, sin has a penalty: "The wages of sin is death" (Rom 6:23).

Deliverance. To free us from the burden of sin, God sent his Son to redeem us. Jesus took the penalty that we deserve for our disobedience and suffered death. The Bible tells us, "There is one God, and there is one mediator between God and men, the man Christ Jesus, who gave himself as a ransom for all" (1 Tim 2:5-6). The Scripture also states that Jesus' death reconciles us to God (Rom 5:8-10). At the Last Supper, Jesus commented on his impending crucifixion: "This is my blood of the covenant, which is poured out for many for the forgiveness of sins" (Mt 26:28). After his death, Jesus rose from the tomb, confirming that he was who he claimed to be and that his payment for sin was complete (Mt 28; Mk 16; Lk 24; Jn 20).

Unlike Rajneesh, Jesus came to give men and women personal and spiritual freedom (Jn 8:36; Gal 5:1). Yet in Christ we do not lose our personality, our individuality. Instead, as individuals we are free to live in relationship to a loving God. We find freedom in a life that is lived in harmony with God, benefiting from his direction and guidance. People like Rajneesh "promise [us] freedom, but they themselves are slaves of corruption" (2 Pet 2:19). Jesus invites us to share the kingdom of his Father, to let "the purpose of the Holy One" be our purpose (Is 5:19).

A Personal Odyssey

Three years ago I walked out on a successful career in West Germany, hoping to find meaning in my life. With a master's degree in business administration, I had been a management trainer for a leading international corporation and later became senior editor of a nationwide business magazine. Upset with the competition I saw, I was seeking a life of straightforwardness and honesty.

In my search, I became acquainted with Rajneesh's teachings. I had read some of his books and knew some people who were living in his ashram. Intrigued with his philosophy, I flew to Poona in 1979.

I had been a sannyasin six months when something extraordinary happened which altered the direction of my life. One night while I was reading in my hotel room, a bright light suddenly appeared. I knew it was Jesus Christ, and he spoke to me in an audible voice. "I want you to become my disciple." I knew immediately that I could follow Rajneesh no longer. Soon thereafter, I severed myself from the movement and since that time have sought to follow Jesus Christ.

When I met Jim, the architect whose story opens this chapter,

I told him what had brought me to Rajneesh: my dissatisfaction with my journalism career, my inability to deal with the terror of life, and my escape to find peace in India. Point by point, we compared Rajneesh's teachings with the words and teachings of Jesus Christ.

Shaking his head, Jim eventually realized that he had been lured by a false view of reality. He had been prepared to accept extinction in place of eternal life. He decided not to join this apocalyptic figure, and Bhagwan's hold on Jim snapped.

To those who have been toying with the quest for mystical enlightenment and who have thought it necessary to seek out a master such as Rajneesh to provide the spiritual techniques for self-realization, I can say that this quest is fruitless. There seems to be no end of gurus and swamis who are willing to accept the mantle of "genuine spiritual master," but the enlightenment they offer is rarely more than a thinly veiled form of self-worship. We are told to bow to the guru's feet, and then we may kneel to our own elusive inner light. For some, this regimen has been exhilarating, even intoxicating; yet for so many people, it proves to be psychologically and spiritually destructive. And as Jesus has so incisively pointed out, the "God" they now worship cannot add one day to the span of life (Mt 6:27).

As God incarnate, Jesus did not merely promise spiritual enlightenment, but demonstrated that he possessed the life he spoke of. He was raised bodily from the grave, as the Bible has recorded. Thus we might know that when he said, "I am the Resurrection and the Life," it was not merely empty rhetoric to impress the gullible. It was the final proof which would separate the deceivers from the divine.

4

Eckankar

Mark Albrecht, Brooks Alexander & Woodrow Nichols

Man will take to religion, even if
he has to invent one.
Paul Twitchell

IN 1964 ANOTHER NEW RELIGION made its appearance on our planet. It was called *Eckankar, The Ancient Science of Soul Travel.*

Today Eckankar is believed to be one of the largest social-religious fringe groups in the United States, if not in the world, with an estimated membership of fifty thousand. It is almost certainly a multimillion dollar organization, thriving on the sale of literature, jewelry and cassette tapes as well as on membership dues. It has recently become much more visible in American culture, putting out storefront signs and advertising in newspapers.

The movement, based in Menlo Park, California, also works actively in Europe, the Middle East, Asia, Australia and Africa. It nevertheless embodies almost all the characteristics of a "made in America" religion. It is an eclectic movement of recent vintage. It combines occult philosophy and mystical experience, big money, misrepresentation of origins, rampant spiritism, psychic manifestations, leader-worship, syncretism, indoctrination and mind control. As in many other new religions, the public image it strives to create differs widely from the inner truths it reveals to initiates.

In twenty years Eckankar has become a highly systematized structure with a large corporate bureaucracy and a resident "God man" as its leader. In almost every respect, it is a perfect example of the spiritual mania characterizing the last two decades. It is a child of our times, an idea whose time has come, a product created to fill a need in our bustling cosmic marketplace. Yet it has kept a low profile, has escaped critical media attention and thus has grown rapidly without impediment.

Paul Twitchell's Ancient Religion
The story of Eckankar is really the story of Paul Twitchell, journalist, occult dabbler and self-proclaimed soldier of fortune, who evolved its philosophy and practice out of his own experience. Twitchell first presented his ideas as a new slant on ancient teachings. In 1964-65 he wrote articles and gave public lectures about his new philosophy of *bilocation* (out-of-the-body travels). As his reputation grew and he attracted a small coterie of disciples, Twitchell began to emphasize the absolute truth of his system. He named his movement *Eckankar*.

More disciples joined, and Twitchell sensed that he had hit upon a winning combination. He then pulled out all the stops, proclaiming himself the unique incarnation of God on earth, insisting that only through him and his movement could an individual find truth. To buttress these claims, he asserted that Eckankar did not begin in 1964 but was rather a timeless and universal truth which had been revived for public dissemination at that time.

He also began to invent his own past. His "biography," *In My Soul I Am Free* by Brad Steiger, agrees only rarely with official documents and family recollections about him.

In spite of his various claims to have been born out of wedlock on a Mississippi riverboat in 1910, 1912 or 1922, Twitchell was really born to Jacob and Effie Twitchell in 1908. He was not raised in "China Point" by a foster mother, as he claimed, but in Paducah, Kentucky, by his own parents. He did not go to Paris or to India but attended Western State Teachers College, wrote poetry, married a home-town girl and joined the U.S. Navy.

After three years in military service Twitchell turned down a promotion, resigned from the Navy and moved with his wife first to New York City and then to Washington, D.C. For several years he did public relations work for an assortment of businesses and agencies. He also began dabbling in Eastern religions.

In 1950 the Twitchells joined Swami Premananda's Self-Revelation Church of Absolute Monism, an offshoot of Paramahansa Yogananda's Self-Realization Fellowship. For several years thereafter they lived on the grounds of the Self-Revelation Church, where Twitchell edited their official publication, *The Mystic Cross*. In 1955, however, Swami Premananda asked him to leave the church. At this time Twitchell also left his wife.

Twitchell soon turned to the ideas of Kirpal Singh, leader of *Ruhani Satsang* ("Divine Science of the Soul"). For several years in the late fifties Twitchell lived in Washington, D.C., and studied Kirpal Singh's teachings and *The Path of the Masters*, a presentation of a similar Eastern philosophy written by fellow Kentuckian Julian Johnson. At the same time Twitchell was a staff member of Scientology. His "biography" nevertheless portrays him as a successful free-lance writer and world traveler during this period.

In the early sixties Twitchell moved to Seattle, where he continued to study and write. He produced a manuscript in 1963 called *The Tiger's Fang*, supposedly an account of wonderful travels taken through the "soul planes" with Kirpal Singh as his guide. In fact it was quite dependent on *The Path of the Masters*, containing many paragraphs lifted virtually verbatim from Johnson's book.

Twitchell sent the manuscript to Kirpal Singh for validation. Kirpal Singh, however, held onto it and warned him not to publish it. That same year Kirpal Singh came to the United States and initiated Twitchell's future second wife, Gail Atkinson, into Ruhani Satsang.

In 1964 Twitchell married Atkinson and broke completely with Kirpal Singh, denying ever having had any association with him. He began to excise Kirpal Singh's name from his writings (the 1967 edition of *The Tiger's Fang*, for example, puts the name "Rebazar Tarzs" in its place). Now independent of his mentor, Twitchell was ready to present Eckankar to the world as a unique and separate movement.

Eckankar's Rod of Power

On October 22, 1965, Rebazar Tarzs supposedly passed the Rod of Power to Twitchell, making him the Mahanta and the 971st Living Eck Master. The new Mahanta began giving public lectures about his "ancient" religion to Southern California audiences. He also published several books and wrote a column for the *New Cosmic Star*.

Eckankar adherents multiplied, and Twitchell established himself as a spiritual leader. He characterized himself as "all powerful, all wise and ... in all places simultaneously. ... The master is a law unto himself."[1]

As the sixties ended, Twitchell faced a problem. According to his earlier teaching, his anointing as Mahanta would expire on October 22, 1970. But Twitchell did not want to give up his exalted position. At the Fourth World-Wide Seminar held in Las Vegas on October 22, 1970, he said nothing about his successor until public pressure forced him to do so. Then he reluctantly explained that those who had been training for the mastership had failed their test. Since new trainees would not be ready for some time, Twitchell would continue as Mahanta for at least another five years.

Not all Eckankar adherents accepted Twitchell's explanation. In January 1971 he tried to silence complaints by explaining that the next Mahanta was still only a child who would not be revealed for at least another fifteen years. Thus if an interval occurred between Twitchell and his successor, Eckankar would be temporarily led by an Eck Master who would not be a Mahanta.[2] In a May 1971 letter to his followers, Twitchell warned that anyone claiming to be the Mahanta without his approval and before the end of the fifteen-year training period would be a deceiver.

But before the end of the year, Twitchell died of a heart attack. Five weeks after his death Eckankar had a new Mahanta. At the Fifth World-Wide Seminar of Eckankar, Gail Atkinson Twitchell announced that the new Mahanta was Darwin Gross, a high-school graduate and self-styled electronics engineer.

Was Gross then a deceiver? Twitchell's widow evidently did not think so. She said that Twitchell had come to her in a dream and revealed his successor. On October 27, 1972, Gail Twitchell married Gross, who described himself as "the only man ever manifested in all of history in whom individualism and universalism are combined in their full expression."[3] Five years later they were divorced.

Ten years after becoming the Mahanta, "the Master, the ruler of the whole world, animate and inanimate,"[4] Gross, at the recommendation of his advisory council (the Ancient Order of the Vairagi), decided to step down. On October 22, 1981, Harold Klemp replaced him as Living Eck Master. Gross, though no longer the Mahanta, continues to lecture as an Eck Master. For the time being, Eckankar has no Mahanta.

Most of these facts would be of little interest or importance were it not for the most important fact of all—the effect of Eckankar on its individual members. Most of Eckankar's estimated fifty thousand members have no idea of the true history of their group. We believe they have committed their lives, their faith and idealism to a false belief system.

The Teachings of Eckankar

Eckankar officially defines itself as the most ancient religious teaching known to man. Its adherents call it "the Path of Total

Awareness" and the "everlasting gospel." It claims to be the way for each individual soul to become "God realized" through the "Ancient Science of Soul Travel."

Eckists are quick to point out that Eckankar is not just another movement. Rather it is "the highest of all movements" and the wellspring from which all religions and philosophies derive whatever portion of truth they have to offer.[5] Twitchell states that "belief in anything except ECK is false," and "it is not possible to enter into the Kingdom of Heaven except through the teachings of ECKANKAR."[6]

Cosmology. The kingdom of heaven to which Twitchell refers is a cosmic layer cake of eleven different realms or planes. Strictly speaking, only the upper six planes are heavenly. The lower five are ruled by the negative God-forces, especially by a cruel buffoon named Kal Niranjan who causes all the woes and confusion we experience here on the earth plane, or first realm.

The second realm, known popularly as the astral plane, gives rise to garden variety occult and psychic phenomena, from deceitful spirits to flying saucers and out-of-the-body astral projection experiences.

Eckankar teaches that few religious disciplines are able to transcend the lower states, due to ignorance and the error of their ways. Only through "soul travel" is one able to flow upward or inward through the various realms in hopes of eventually reaching the *Sugmad* (God), which exists as pure formless essence on the topmost plane.

The journey is not easy. Only by submitting to the guidance of the Living Eck Master, or Mahanta, one can succeed. The Mahanta plugs the *chela* (disciple) into the cosmic current, the *Eck*, which flows out from and back into the Sugmad. Eckists say the Eck can be heard and seen. Thus with the help of the Mahanta, other spirit guides and two of his five senses, the chela learns to flow with the Eck up through the various planes, gradually attaining enlightenment and spiritual maturity along the way.

God. There is much talk about God in the writings of Eckankar.

The religion teaches that God is all things, which is fundamentally the view found in orthodox Vedantic Hinduism. Unlike standard Eastern monism, however, Eckankar teaches that the individual soul is not extinguished when it merges with the Absolute. Each individual soul becomes a "coworker" with God and retains its individuality to some extent. Yet "there is nothing in the universe that is not the SUGMAD, the everlasting ECK."[7]

If God is all things, that by definition includes the negative entities and energies in the universe such as Kal Niranjan, tyrant of the lower worlds. Kal's purpose is to mislead and deceive. He controls and defrauds souls in reincarnation after reincarnation, trapping them in a web of attachment and illusion like a giant spider. Yet though Kal is inexorably set against the will of the Sugmad, he is of one essence with it.

Kal "is only a lower manifestation of God, although he is free to do as he likes, but his general orders are given from above."[8] Like all monistic belief systems, Eckankar cannot avoid pinning the universe's flaws upon its own God, and Eckists grudgingly admit that the Sugmad's "lower natures" generate negativity. Eckankar tries to evade this dilemma by teaching that evil results from abused free will which spawns ignorance and leads to a lack of God-realization in the self.

Sin and salvation. Concepts of blame and personal culpability do creep into Eckankar. While the Eck power is mysteriously "above the dichotomy of good and evil," hapless individual souls are not.[9] As souls live their lives and make both conscious and unconscious choices, they accrue *karma* and *karmic debt.* Souls must pay for or work off karmic debt acquired through wrong action either in this life or in a previous one.

Karmic debt piles up quickly when one engages in any of the *five passions:* lust, anger, greed, undue attachment to material things, and vanity. The individual soul must go through a seemingly endless round of reincarnations to work off karma—though the Catch-22 is that even more karma is acquired in the process. This can take millions of years and thousands, even millions, of reincarnations as the soul rises up the evolutionary scale of life.

Eckankar teaches that a soul enters the universe as a mineral and works its way up through plant, fish, reptile and mammal incarnations. When it eventually becomes human, it will spend any number of lifetimes until it attains spiritual enlightenment through Eckankar. If a soul abuses the spiritual light it has attained, it is sent back to start over again in a lower form.

According to Eckankar, the short cut to God-realization is to meet and follow a Living Eck Master, whose presence will burn away eons of karmic debt, freeing the soul from endless rebirths. There is always an Eck Master on earth to liberate the floundering masses. The current Living Eck Master is Sri Harold Klemp. His three predecessors—Darwin Gross, Paul Twitchell and Rebazar Tarzs (a five-hundred-year-old Tibetan monk created by Twitchell)—are considered a step above most Masters. They were *Mahantas*, full incarnations of the Sugmad, possessing all divine attributes within a human body, reputedly able to lift people out of the cycle of death and rebirth if they submit in total faith and self-negation.

Spiritual practice. Due to the pre-eminent place of the Mahantas, spiritual practice often revolves around them. Since they are the distilled essence of the divine life-current, Eck disciples focus their attention on them in their spiritual exercises by contemplating either their physical or their "inner" (spiritual) form. Eck centers may be adorned with a Mahanta's portrait.

While the movement disavows overt worship of the Mahantas, a public-relations flyer published when Darwin Gross was Mahanta called him "the Vi-Guru, the Light-Giver, the Way Shower, the protector, guide and companion of every ECK chela," as well as "the sole authority of Eckankar's doctrine." Further, Eckankar scripture states that "the faith that one has in the Mahanta must be that of complete understanding and surrender."

The primary spiritual exercise is soul travel or out-of-the-body experiences. Five of the major techniques used are imaginative projection, meditation, projection via the dream state, trance, and

66

direct projection or intentionally willing one's consciousness to be in another location. Mantras are frequently chanted, and contact with spirit guides is practiced. In fact, almost all forms and types of occult mystical consciousness-alteration come into play.

Spiritual practice grows more esoteric as the Eckist travels up through the realms. There are up to ten initiations, one for advancement to each plane. These are generally given yearly and are considered the basic holy rite of Eckankar.

A Christian Response

Eckankar's God. Twitchell early realized that if he was going to create a new religion, he had to conjure up a new concept of God to go with it. He came up with a hybrid, blending monism and pantheism with a touch of monotheism to give his theology some character. The final product is a confused, crippled and impotent deity. Like most hybrids, the Sugmad is sterile, incapable of producing new life.

Identified totally with all things in creation, visible or invisible, the god of Eckankar does not have personality. Consequently, according to Twitchell, "we do not, and cannot, know God."[10] Obviously this kind of god is unconcerned with humanity and the plight of the individual. Twitchell writes: "God of Itself is not interested in the individual and his cause, but only the continuation of life."[11]

Twitchell also dismisses the concept of a transcendent God: "To say God created the universe and then to say that he stands outside the universe is a contradiction." He does not explain why these statements are incompatible, though he attempts to justify his assertion with the pronouncement that "neither God nor no-God can exist outside this oneness."[12]

The God of the Bible, by contrast, is Creator of the universe (Gen 1:1). He is personal: he loves the human beings he has created and he communicates with them. The Bible itself is one way God communicates with people (2 Tim 3:16). An even more important way is through his own unique Incarnation, Jesus Christ, who is the living union of God and humanity (Jn 1:1-18).

The God of the Bible is also supremely moral. He is entirely good; evil is completely foreign to his nature (Ex 34:6-7; Ps 5:4; Hab 1:13). Evil, according to the Bible, results from rebellion against God (Gen 3). Although God allows evil to exist for a while, he will not tolerate it forever (Rev 20:10, 13-15).

Compare these biblical concepts with Eckankar's concept of God's morality. Twitchell says that there is "a conflict between the righteousness of God and the wrongness of Kal,"[13] yet Kal "is only a lower manifestation of God."[14] "The Kal is also a part of God's own divine power."[15]

Where does that leave us? In Eckist theology, the Sugmad is not only directly responsible for the existence of evil and falsehood, it actually embodies these characteristics. If this were true, the universe would be a place of eternal despair and trickery and we would never be able to place our faith in the Sugmad. At best, such a God is capricious and fickle; at worst, inherently and incurably malignant.

Yet how can the God of the Bible be both loving and moral when the very people he loves are so often immoral? The Bible teaches that Jesus, God's Son, lived, died and rose from the dead in our place and for us (Rom 5:6-11; Col 2:8-15). Jesus offers us his life so that we may live forever in God's presence (Jn 3:16; Heb 9:24). The loving God of the Bible provides the way to reconcile us to himself and at the same time to destroy the evil that is making our present lives difficult, even though this way of reconciliation involved much pain to himself. This is true love indeed.

By contrast, in The Tiger's Fang Twitchell describes the Sugmad as ignorant, internally inconsistent, in need of wisdom and education, negative, unawakened, poor, unhappy, not content with creation and in need of assistance. In a final burst, he lapses into blasphemy: "God is hideous, forbidding, frightening, shocking, pretentious, garish, unprepossessing, ugly, plain, coarse, distorted, unbeautiful, and about any of the adjectives one wants to use in describing that part of Him as power."[16]

One of the red flags of any false belief system is a low view of God. This is not surprising when one considers the source of false religion—Satan himself. The Bible tells us that since the beginning he has set himself squarely against God and his plans and purposes. At the heart of every lie he perpetrates on gullible humans is an untrue representation of God, a swipe at God's character and attributes.

Concerning Satan, Jesus said, "He was a murderer from the beginning, and has nothing to do with the truth, because there is no truth in him. When he lies, he speaks according to his own nature, for he is a liar and the father of lies" (Jn 8:44). Indeed, in all of Satan's counterfeits God is represented as imperfect in one way or another, for the devil cannot tell the truth about God.

Eckankar's spirituality. In Eckankar, as in many contemporary cults, subjective spiritual experience rather than logical thinking validates a member's participation in the group. People are often undiscerning in spiritual matters. The Bible teaches that humanity, though created perfect, chose to disobey God and therefore "fell" into a state of imperfection and sin (Gen 3; Rom 5:12-21). None of us is free from the effects of that Fall; our very nature has been damaged (Is 53:6; Rom 3:10-18). As a result, we have all come into the world with dormant spiritual faculties. As we grow older our apathy and naiveté are reinforced by interaction and preoccupation with the material world. Consequently, when a person with minimal discernment of good and evil spiritual forces has a psychic experience, whether a flash of intuitive illumination, contact with familiar spirits or some type of ESP, he or she usually accepts the experience as true or valid simply because it happened. The possibility that a transcendent experience may be both real and deceptive is seldom considered.

Twitchell constantly emphasized the importance of experience as one of the foundations of Eckankar. He wrote, "Eck does not depend on books, nor waste its time on discussions of what truth is, or God Itself. What Eck demands of its Chela is to enter into the center of the Supreme Reality and to learn for himself."[17]

This learning experience is derived from interaction with the spirit realms and altered states of consciousness. Eckankar's discourses for chelas give detailed instructions for entering into these states, usually through sensory deprivation and focusing of attention on a mantra (word) or some spiritual form.

Undoubtedly many Eckist experiences are a cultivated and amplified form of daydream or fantasy. The "imaginative technique" for soul travel is the first of the five methods used to transcend the body. Twitchell's writings frequently stress the importance of imagination and detailed fantasy.

While imagination and fantasy combined with altered states of consciousness may account for most of the average chela's spiritual experience, actual contact with spiritual entities is probably the strongest factor in validating the teachings of Eckankar for the participant. Eckankar encourages trance states and spiritism from the outset:

> I give you a simple beginner's exercise which will help you get out of the body and travel briefly in the first plane. Just before going to bed at night, sit in an easy chair or on the floor, concentrating your attention on the spiritual eye—the place between the eyebrows, and chant the word AUM, or God, or some short spiritual verse. Meanwhile the attention should be put on the inner form of the teacher, if you have one, and if not you can put it on Christ, or any great spiritual master, and even if you wish on the writer of this discourse. All of a sudden you will be outside the body in company of the other entity who will take you on a short journey. . . . No harm will come to you.[18]

In contrast to this indiscriminate welcoming of spiritual entities, the Bible warns, "Beloved, do not believe every spirit, but test the spirits to see whether they are of God; for many false prophets have gone out into the world. By this you know the Spirit of God: every spirit which confesses that Jesus Christ has come in the flesh is of God, and every spirit which does not confess Jesus is not of God. This is the spirit of antichrist" (1 Jn 4:1-3).

Contact with spirits and disembodied entities of all sorts is an integral part of Eck's spiritual practice. Yet despite Twitchell's warnings about harmful spiritual beings, he throws caution to the wind and routinely assumes that whatever entity comes along will be at least innocuous if not actually helpful. The Mahanta supposedly manifests himself as a ball of blue light: "A flesh-and-blood man, as the Outer Master, he is also seen on the inner screens as a blue light, a globe of blue or white light, a ball of light, a tiny or large blue star, as the Inner Master."[19] Twitchell says that "the Master appears often as the Blue Star, and sometimes as a misty, pale blue light. The Star or the Light will lead the chela gently onward through the various planes into the Soul region. He must trust it completely, never being doubtful or hesitant about following it, nor wondering where it may lead him."[20]

Trusting a hazy blue spirit manifestation just because someone says it is the Mahanta hardly seems a judicious thing to do. In fact, it is dangerous. According to the esoteric teaching of witchcraft, Lucifer's demonic hordes are organized in an ethereal color code. Certain of them appear as luminous beings of various colors. Experiences involving the color blue seem to be particularly common in spiritistic and occult lore.

The deeper we look into the spiritual practice of Eckankar, the more obvious it becomes that disciples are interacting with demonic elements. Biblical warnings about "doctrines of demons" (1 Tim 4:1) are more than metaphorical admonitions. Twitchell gives a startling insight into the spiritual mechanics of Eckankar in a discourse on psychic transmission:

There are two main techniques which are used knowingly or unknowingly, which the transmitter adopts. They are the trance, one in which the communicator [the spirit guide] or the entity's power uses the mind, by shutting off the thoughts and making it blank. It then takes advantage of this condition and uses it as a vehicle to pass the message on to the audience on the outer plane.

The other method is etheric telepathy. This is often known as mind-to-mind contact, a state in which the entity uses its power and force to inject ideas into the medium's mind with the medium's own consciousness being withdrawn.[21]

It is apparent that the Eckankar disciple's mystical travels into other realms are likely to be no more than a spiritual telecast implanted into his or her blank mind.

Despite the fact that trance mediumship is central to Eck spiritual practice, Twitchell sometimes warns that mediumship and trance states are harmful to spiritual development. His warnings, however, seem to be cosmetic attempts to elevate Eckankar above other occult practices and to be consistent with his warnings about harmful spirits on the astral plane.

In fact, the trance state is one of his prescribed techniques for getting out of the body and establishing spiritual contact. Furthermore, although he often contends that bizarre spiritual experiences or manifestations of psychic phenomena are spiritual distractions to be avoided, this also appears to be an attempt to cover up the real source of Eckankar's spiritual experience. It appears that Twitchell wants to use the undeniable spiritual power of trance mediumship while dissociating himself from its bad reputation. In truth, he encourages many types of occult practices.

In a writing titled "The Thirty-two Facets of Eckankar," Twitchell says that "while traveling the road to the true Godhead via ECK, the chela finds himself going through thirty-two varied but unique phases of spiritual unfoldment, including mediumship, ESP, telepathy, mind reading, clairvoyance, magic, cosmic consciousness, alchemy and weather control.[22]

Despite the many different varieties of spiritual and psychic control used in Eckankar, the experiences do not always take place during the exercises. Twitchell concedes that an experience can also be totally negative, though he writes this off as a "Kal" experience. Admitting that the entities often can't be trusted, he says that "many astral forms which are wandering around pestering human beings are concerned with either hatred or sorrow."[23]

In reality, it is not the fictitious Kal Niranjan that generates these experiences but supernatural entities bent on the deception and ultimate destruction of the chela. Twitchell observes: "There will be times when he wonders at his own actions because they seem so strange. . . . He is both powerful and yet helpless in the sense that his actions are all now directed by the Mahanta and his own will cannot enter into the acts which are performed."[24] Nevertheless Eckists are exhorted to "sell their souls" to the Mahanta and the movement, and chelas are informed that "one must surrender himself completely to this feeling [of total control by the Mahanta] until his whole being is possessed by it."[25]

Eckists must ask themselves if it is safe to trust the guidance of any spirit, even if it claims to be the Mahanta. The Bible forthrightly warns that spiritual deception may present itself in appealing, pleasurable forms: "For even Satan disguises himself as an angel of light" (2 Cor 11:14).

A perfunctory study of spiritism reveals that the favorite game of demons is masquerading as something or someone else. How does one distinguish between the blue star of the Mahanta and the annihilating blue mist of Satan himself?

The spirit of Eckankar. Retired Mahanta Darwin Gross insists that "the individual in ECKANKAR is not brainwashed for ECKANKAR and Its teachings are not a cult or sect in any way."[26] But a sampling of Twitchell's writings seem to contradict this.

1. Eckists must not question what they are taught. "We must not spend time and effort in reading other books outside ECK, and taking courses from others because it only tends to bring on confusion. . . . The fewer questions the chela asks the better off he will be. . . . The chela must not make judgments of the Master nor of his words."[27]

2. Eckists must give up their minds to another's control. "Complete surrender to the ECK Master is the only path to total freedom."[28] "It is not always the ECKist either that finds the deeper secrets, but only those . . . who are willing to surrender and sacrifice themselves to the Mahanta." The Eckist "is both powerful and yet helpless in the sense that his actions are all now directed

by the Mahanta and his own will cannot enter into the acts which are performed."[29]

3. Eckists must never think of leaving Eckankar. "Once any ECKist becomes a member of the Second Initiation and beyond, ... he cannot ever resign from ECK.... If such persons ... ever attempt to resign or want to leave ECK for any purpose, they shall find it not easy to do.... [They] will run into terrible problems."[30]

Such a system is totally incompatible with the Christian religion. The Bible encourages believers to "test the spirits" (1 Jn 4:1), in fact, to "test everything" (1 Thess 5:21). Christian evangelists appealed to people's reasoning powers: "Paul went in, as was his custom, and for three weeks he argued with them from the scriptures, explaining and proving" (Acts 17:2-3a). They exhorted believers to explain their faith intelligently: "Always be prepared to make a defense to any one who calls you to account for the hope that is in you" (1 Pet 3:15).

If Eckankar's method is incompatible with Christianity, its message is even more so. Eckankar's claim to be "the only direct path to God"[31] collides head-on with Jesus' assertion, "No one comes to the Father, but by me" (Jn 14:6).

The apostle John warned that "every spirit which does not confess Jesus is not of God. This is the spirit of antichrist" (1 Jn 4:3). The apostle Peter confessed, "You are the Christ, the Son of the living God" (Mt 16:16). By contrast, Twitchell said, "We really see [Jesus] as a son of Kal Niranjan, king of the lower worlds."[32]

We might ponder John's observation: "And this is the judgment, that the light has come into the world, and men loved darkness rather than light, because their deeds were evil" (Jn 3:19).

For the thousands who have been initiated into Eckankar and others who have been influenced by Twitchell's prolific pen, we hope this survey has been helpful. If it provides a basis for deep reflection and self-examination or reality testing, it will have achieved our objective.

5

est

John Weldon

*Life is always perfect just
the way it is.*
Werner Erhard

GERRY, A REAL-ESTATE SALESMAN, says, "I'm more confident
and aware in dealing with people. I can look them in the eye,
literally and figuratively."[1]

Dr. Richard M. Dawes, a clinical assistant professor in the
Department of Psychiatry at Louisiana State University, writes,
"I've seen it work with myself, my patients and my friends. I have
broken through so many barriers, for both myself and my patients,
that I can only be high about it."[2]

Felice, a young Hispanic-American from Brooklyn, says, "I was
afraid of everything. People, the dark, bugs, animals, crowded
rooms, open spaces. . . . Now my desire to kill myself is gone. . . .
I'm not afraid anymore . . . of anything."[3]

Another graduate says, "It changed my relationship with my husband. . . . It turned me around 180 degrees and I can finish things I

never could before, like doing the dishes before I go to work."[4]

Others report that they have rid themselves of medical problems, can lose weight without trying, are getting better jobs and forming better relationships, and are feeling better about money, sex and God.[5] What has caused these dramatic improvements in their lives? They all point to Werner Erhard and his intensive 60-hour training program called est. Erhard Seminars Training (though est is also Latin for "it is") is the major thrust of the est organization that recently changed its name to Werner Erhard and Associates.

A Powerful Growth Experience

From 1971 to 1981 est trained over 325,000 people in thirty-five cities in the United States, Europe, the Middle East and Asia with more than 50,000 others participating each year.[6] Up to three hundred people at a time are trained during two consecutive weekends, usually in a hotel ballroom, at a current cost of $400 each. Erhard has initiated an instruction program that he hopes will yield an additional ninety to a hundred trainers by 1983.[7] Since only nine trainers taught the first 160,000 graduates from 1971 to 1978, est seems prepared for tremendous expansion.

The official stated purpose of the est training "is to transform your ability to experience living so that the situations you have been trying to change or have been putting up with, clear up just in the process of life itself."

Among the est graduates are a number of celebrities such as Yoko Ono, Carly Simon, gold medalist John Curry, Joanne Woodward, Polly Bergen and Diana Ross. John Denver wrote a song about est ("Looking for Space") and dedicated it to Erhard. Another graduate, Jerry Rubin, states, "It addresses itself to basic human needs, and does work by giving people a greater sense of themselves. In many ways, it was the most powerful growth experience I had."[8]

The est advisory boards have included Don Cox (former vice president and director of planning for Coca-Cola, USA), Roger Sant (former assistant administrator, Federal Energy Administration), Jack Thayer (president, NBC radio), Richard Aurelio (former deputy mayor of New York City) and other highly placed people.

What is est? How did est gather such a following? Where did it come from?

Werner Erhard

To answer these questions we must begin with the founder of est. Werner Erhard was born John Paul (Jack) Rosenberg in Philadelphia on September 5, 1935. His formal education ended in 1952 when he graduated from high school. He changed his name after he abandoned his wife and four children in 1960 (he made amends thirteen years later). He headed for St. Louis with a woman named Ellen, who became his second wife.

Later in Spokane he sold the Great Books and in 1963 joined the Parents Cultural Institute, a subsidiary of *Parents Magazine*, whose only business was selling encyclopedias door to door. He became a vice president responsible for training and supervising salesmen. When PCI went out of business in 1969, Erhard joined Grolier Society, Inc., as a division manager.

During his stay with Grolier, Erhard met several people in the San Francisco human-potential movement, one of whom was Dr. Leo Zeff, an LSD researcher who is now on est's advisory board. He and others led Erhard to Scientology, a controversial religious movement offering total spiritual freedom to all followers through its "spiritual technology."[9] Erhard was also closely associated with Alex Everett, founder of Mind Dynamics, a self-hypnosis mind-control enterprise specializing in developing psychic powers.[10]

About three years after leaving his family, Erhard had a radical life-transforming experience of enlightenment while driving his car down Highway 101 in Marin County, California. That experience was eventually to culminate (via other transformations and research) in the seminars training.

W. W. Bartley's biography of Erhard indicates extensive psycho-spiritual and occult involvement on Erhard's part prior to starting

---

77

est.[11] Besides Scientology and Mind Dynamics, Erhard studied or became involved in Zen Buddhism (he has made trips to the East to study with Zen masters), hypnosis, Subud, Yoga (he was one of Swami Muktananda's original sponsors in the U.S.), Silva Mind Control, psychocybernetics, Gestalt, encounter therapy and transpersonal psychology. Est is the fruit of his "conversion" experience and personal research into those and other disciplines.[12]

Out of the two-weekend est training itself have grown a number of associated organizations. The est-sponsored Hunger Project has a membership of almost two million. Its goal is to wipe out hunger by 1997. The est Foundation gives charitable grants for research, communication, education and studies in human well-being and transformation. The Holiday Project was set up to visit hospital patients and prison inmates and give them gifts during the Christmas/Hanukkah season. The Breakthrough Foundation, the Community Workshop and the Center for Contextual Study are also connected with est. More than 20,000 people volunteer their time to these various est projects each year.[13] Most of these had their initial contact with est through the seminars training. Stewart Emery's Actualizations and John Hanley's Lifespring are both offshoots of est which are not, however, officially related to it. Their graduates together total about 200,000.

What Happens at the est Training?

How do the seminars transform so many people into such enthusiastic supporters of est? An interesting combination of techniques is used. Promptly at 8:30 the first Saturday morning a training supervisor goes over the ground rules four or five times: no talking, no smoking, no note-taking, no watches allowed in the seminar room, no sitting next to anyone you knew before you came, no getting out of the chair except for one food break and three bathroom breaks during each sixteen-hour day. Between weekends, trainees agree not to take any alcohol or drugs (except as prescribed by a doctor).

Then onto the stage strides the trainer dressed like Erhard in a sport coat, open collar, slacks and sleek shoes. Adelaide Bry describes the first moments this way: "He wasted no time in getting down to business. There were no introductions, no preliminaries, no niceties. He glowered at us and announced that we were all assholes. I knew it was coming but I flinched anyway. A woman in front of me began to shake."[14] The trainer proceeds to tell the trainees that they are machines. Their lives don't work. All their best strategies, theories, beliefs and hopes about what is true and helpful in life is so much cow manure. The trainer paces and accuses, continually peppering his speech with profanity.

Trainees are allowed to respond by raising their hands. A volunteer will rush a microphone to a person who is recognized. Many, of course, raise objections to what is being said. But the trainer relentlessly kids or curses each one into seeing that no belief system works. "Understanding is the booby prize" is a favorite Erhard aphorism. Intellectuals, already guilty of thinking, are caught in a Catch-22: "All criticism is self-created and says more about the critic than the subject discussed."[15]

Gradually the trainer moves into another major thrust of the est system. We are totally responsible for everything that happens in our lives. If your mother died when you were young, it's your fault. If you were laid off, you've only yourself to blame. Being born with a brain tumor is no excuse. Again objections are dispatched or handled with "I got that," which in est does not mean the trainer agrees with the statement but that he realizes the significance of a communication.

As the hours pass, backaches, full bladders, hunger, nausea and boredom set in. Some trainees begin asking for the est vomit bags. Complaints grow. The trainer shows then how est can overcome these through "processes." Experience the pain fully. Enter into it. See it. And one by one people testify that the pain is gone.[16] The last hours of the first day (midnight to 3:00 A.M.) end with more training in processes. Trainees are told to close their eyes, enter a meditation state and journey to an idyllic beach. In a monotone the trainer drones the instructions, "Create a space in your left foot. . . . Good. . . . Create a space in your left foot. . . . Thank you. . . . Create a space in your left foot. . . . Good."[17] The group is then sent home bleary eyed and exhausted with the promise of the Truth Process the next day.

Sunday begins at 10:15 A.M. Sometimes the temperature in the hotel ballroom is set in the low 40s. The verbal abuse continues. Eventually, time for the Truth Process arrives. The chairs are all moved from their precise rows to the edges of the room. Trainees are instructed to lie on the floor and concentrate on one big problem in their lives they want to solve. Over a three-hour period they are told to focus on different parts of their bodies and then on the problem itself, what it feels like, the images and events associated with it, the bodily sensations and emotions. Bry writes, "His directions continued, and the scene grew noisy; an incredible cacophony of sound erupted as each one of the two hundred and fifty men and women, lying flat on their backs on the floor of the giant ballroom, went into their 'item.' Two hundred and fifty people in every form of emotion, giving free vent to vomiting, shaking, sobbing, hysterical laughing, raging—re-creating experience in a safe space. No one paid the slightest attention to anyone else."[18] Convulsing bodies, flailing limbs, deafening whoops of pain and pleasure rise to a crescendo. By the end most are convinced they have gone through a deeply cleansing experience.

After dinner the trainees are commanded to go on the stage, row by row, and stand at attention to be examined by the rest of the group for what is called the Danger Process. "It would be difficult to imagine the tension and fear that Tony [the trainer] and his assistants were able to whip up over this objectively ridiculous exercise."[19]

William Greene, author of *Est: Four Days to Make Your Life Work*, describes it this way:

The first row is told to go to the platform and make eye contact. Watching this Process is somewhat like being transmitted to a combination insane asylum/torture ward. What happens to the trainees is absolutely incredible. . . . Like a scene from a horror movie, people began to fall apart right before your eyes. The man who had never been able to tell his wife that he really needed her went into a catatonic state. The woman who confessed to never having an orgasm cried until she collapsed. A young man, who had come with his married sister, cried hysterically. A tall, thin man swayed like a willow in the wind. Finally, he fainted on the floor. The trainer ran over and started screaming at him. "Cut the act, Michael. That's just a big game you're playing."[20]

The first weekend concludes with another process in which the chairs are again stacked and everyone is flat on the floor. All are told to imagine they are terrified of the persons next to them. Next they are afraid of all those around them and then the entire room. Soon the enemy is the city, and finally the whole world is out to murder them. Again the room fills with shrieks and writhing bodies as the imagined horror becomes all too real.

The process ends when the trainer brings the group back to reality by telling them the Big Joke. If they were afraid of everyone in the room, then everyone in the room—indeed, the world—must be afraid of them. A sense of power dawns on the group, and giggles of relief replace the cries of terror. It is about 3:00 A.M., and the trainees march ecstatically out into the darkness with their newfound power over everyone else in the world.

A midweek training divides the two weekends, an evening during which testimonies are heard on how est has changed lives and encouragement is given to the rest to stick with it until they "get it."

The Second Weekend
The second weekend is like the first. Long periods between breaks. Long lectures on the nature of reality and the anatomy of the mind. More talk on how their lives don't work. More processes guide trainees to put themselves inside a daisy, a cherry tomato and a strawberry. " 'You're part of every atom in the world and every atom is part of you.' We are all gods who created our own worlds."[21] More commands to not try to figure est out, to realize

that what they will get out of est is nothing, that the reason it takes sixty hours to "get" nothing is that "you have to move through all the somethings you're stuck with to get to nothing."[22]

Finally, late on Sunday comes the fulfillment of the promise that they will "get it." " 'I'll tell you everything there is to know about life,' the trainer said on that final day. 'What is, is, and what ain't, ain't. Enlightenment,' he continued, 'is knowing you are a machine. *You are a machine.*' "[23] Mark Brewer described the next moments this way:

> Then came the miracle. If you accept the nature of your mind, Ted [the trainer] explained with a rising optimism in his voice, and take responsibility for having created all the stimulus-response mechanisms it comprises, then in effect you have freely chosen to do everything you have ever done and to be precisely what you are. In that instant, you become exactly what you always wanted to be! ... The light dawned slowly, with Ted chirping, "See? See?" and then one and another acknowledged eagerly that, yes, they got it, and gradually a swell of exultant revelation swept the place. It was amazing to behold. They were perfect exactly the way they were.[24]

How Do They Get It?

The effect is euphoria as the vast majority of trainees "get it" each est seminar, and thousands move on to volunteer their time for the cause, pay about $50 for graduate seminars such as "About Sex," "Be Here Now" and "What's So," and recruit friends and relatives for the est training itself with evangelistic zeal. How did they "get it"—and such enthusiasm along with it?

The est general information brochure states that est "is not like group therapy, sensitivity training, encounter groups, positive thinking, meditation, hypnosis, mind control, behavior modification, or psychology. In fact, est is not therapy and is not psychology." Rather it is considered educational and philosophical in nature. Dr. Sheridan Fenwick, however, refers to one interchange between a trainer and a trainee.

He made her go through a whole routine that she was in fact responsible for her brother's death, that she had killed him. The trainer was . . . saying that it was her fault. She protested and said she hadn't forced her brother, she hadn't held the gun to his head or pulled the trigger. The trainer kept after her, insisting that she was responsible for the death, and finally she was crying and saying yes, that she had killed her brother. . . .

You could say this wasn't psychotherapy, in the best sense of the word. I'm certainly not saying that I think these people were necessarily helped. . . . Est may not be psychotherapy, but I find it unbelievable that it could be considered to be "education" or some kind of philosophical training. Is education supposed to concern itself with guilt over a brother's suicide?

Is est psychotherapy? If it walks like a duck, and talks like a duck, then it might well be a platypus. But the odds are, if you're not at the zoo, it's a duck.[25]

Brainwashing?

Some have gone further to suggest that in addition to using techniques from psychotherapy and hypnosis, a form of brainwashing is used to achieve the profound effects of the est training. It could certainly not be classified under the same type of brainwashing used by the North Koreans during the Korean War, which used torture with extreme and continued physical-sensory deprivation. However, Hinsie and Campbell define *menticide* (popularly known as "brainwashing") as "an organized system of psychological intervention and judicial perversion in which a powerful tyrant synthetically injects his own thoughts and words into the minds and mouths of the victims he plans to destroy by mock trial."[26]

Perhaps implicit in that statement is the idea of involuntary confinement, something not true of est. People do choose to go and do choose to stay. Indeed several times during each seminar the trainer offers their money back if they want to leave right then. But authoritarian atmosphere works against anyone taking such offers.

In *Psychology Today* Mark Brewer writes, "Such efforts are commonly known as brainwashing, which is precisely what the est experience is, and the result is usually a classic conversion."[27] In the same issue, San Francisco State professor Richard P. Marsh presents the case for est. He says it is not brainwashing, defining brainwashing as an attempt "to confuse by sudden reversals of logic, to frighten and humiliate a captive subject in order to break his will and insinuate forcibly into his mind the belief system of his captor."[28] From what we have observed, he is for the most part describing est.

Greene remarks, "Everyone goes through a tremendous emotional upheaval. During that upheaval, the belief systems of the trainees are very often cast aside."[29] Heck and Thompson concur: "A major step in the est training is negating any pre-existing belief system."[30] And one est trainer told his trainees, "We're gonna throw away your whole belief system.... We're gonna tear you down and put you back together."[31]

The question of brainwashing seems to depend on the degree of force and coercion used to effect the change in beliefs. The evidence seems to indicate that est should be labeled a mild form of brainwashing, or at least intensive indoctrination. Even pro-est writers have acknowledged the controversy. Luke Rhinehart, for example, notes that in his mind the most substantial argument against est so far is "that the training is a form of brainwashing," although he feels that this is not the case.[32] Even Erhard says that the est techniques are "mind blowing": "You give it (the mind) something that it's incapable of handling."[33]

Intellect alone cannot easily withstand the onslaught of the training. Intellectual attackers often become yielded converts. Dr. Kovel remarks:

> The most sophisticated judgment is no match for such seminar conditions—which indeed make their effect felt, not on the intellect, but on the soft space that yearning occupies behind the mask of reason. Numerous people who have undergone est tell how they attempted to dispute the trainer, only to become con-

founded and yield. What such reports leave out is that the most powerful intellect necessarily becomes puerile under the conditions of the training. It is like playing tennis with your side of the court under water.[34]

The first published study in professional literature on the harmful effects of est training can be found in the March and November 1977 issues of the *American Journal of Psychiatry*.[35] The two-part study considers seven cases. Six developed psychotic reactions after the training (some of them life-threatening), although five had no previous psychiatric illness or treatment themselves or in their family histories. Thus there is no guarantee that any person who takes est will be free from psychotic reactions. While the doctors emphasize that no direct cause-effect link between est and serious psychopathology can be proven without further systematic study, "there's enough possibility of a real connection between est and psychotic breaks to cause us to want to alert psychiatrists and psychologists."

What Do They Get?

If est is so successful at removing any beliefs one might have before going into the training, what do they replace them with? One of the main tenets of est is one mentioned before: each of us is totally responsible for our lives. As one Berkeley student said after her est training, "What makes all the difference in my life is that I am in control and that I choose the kind of experiences that I am having."[36] We can't blame others for mistakes or ill fortune. We are in total control of all that happens to us, and whatever happiness or sorrow we experience is what we have chosen to happen. Therefore, right now our lives must be exactly what we want them to be. As Erhard has said, "Life is always perfect just the way it is."[37]

Essentially, what this means is that our own experiences create ultimate reality. Objective truth is an illusion. The fact that a large group of people might hold to the same truth (such as that Canada is north of the United States) is simply an agreement that has no basis in reality except as people experience it. Such agreements allow society to function, but they only symbolize final reality—our experience.

This puts truth beyond the realm of belief or thinking or logic. As Erhard has said, "Understanding is the booby prize." We experience truth. We don't learn it.

Having gone this far, est does not retreat from the implications of such statements. For if we create ultimate reality, we are nothing less than God. Indeed, in his book on est, in which "each page ... [was] checked by an est trainer" to ensure accuracy,[38] Luke Rhinehart says Erhard's view is that "human beings [are] God," and he quotes a trainer as saying, "In actuality, each of us, as the sole creator of our universe, is a God."[39] Other est graduates testify to the same view: "You are God and you create everything around you and you create the universe."[40] And, "You are in effect recognizing your own Godhood."[41]

This is essentially an Eastern concept of God. God is all that exists. Everything is a part of God. Anything that is not a part of God is illusion or maya. The goal of most yoga in Hinduism is to realize that one is not a body. The body, the self (ego), is unreal. The real person is Self, Brahman (the essence of the whole cosmos), or the Absolute. And according to Erhard, my Self equals your Self equals the same Self. All is One. "Self is all there is. I mean, that's it. To pay attention to personality is to pay attention to an illusion."[42]

Erhard has acknowledged his indebtedness to the East many times. He has called Zen Buddhism and Scientology the most influential forces in formulating est.[43] Many of the grants of the est Foundation have gone to occult and Eastern religious groups or movements like the Naropa (Tibetan Buddhist) Institute in Colorado and Nyingma Center in Berkeley, the San Francisco Zen Center, and funded presentations by the Dalai Lama.[44] Est also sponsored a recent U.S. tour of the Hindu guru Swami Muktananda and Tibetan Buddhist XVI Gyalwa Karmpa. Jerry Rubin says, "Est is an important part in the easternization of America."[45]

Erhard claims that est doesn't interfere with anyone's religious beliefs, but says, "Had I been in any religious order, or any church or monastery, I definitely could not have done any of this. It would have been heresy."[54] On another occasion Erhard put it more clearly: "For instance, I believe that 'belief' in God is the greatest barrier to God in the universe—the single greatest barrier. I would prefer someone who is ignorant to someone who believes in God. Because the belief in God is a total barrier, almost a total barrier to God. . . . There isn't anything but spirituality, which is just another word for God, because God is everything."[55]

A Contrast to Christianity

Although a Christian believer would be told that est would not interfere with his or her religious beliefs, that is not true. The est belief system is designed to destroy the validity of the Christian world view and every other world view one might have prior to the training. Est is supposedly nonreligious, but since its purpose is to alter one's epistemology and instill a monistic or pantheistic belief in impersonal divinity, est qualifies as religious. In the est philosophy, Christianity is detrimental to growth and enlightenment. "In est training you are God. . . . Therefore you cannot look to any supreme being for special treatment, goodness, or award."[56]

The biblical world view paints a startlingly different picture of reality. Genesis 1—2 makes it abundantly clear that God created the universe and all that is in it. We are his creatures, his created ones. The opening of John's Gospel makes the same point: "In the beginning was the Word, and the Word was with God, and the Word was God. He was in the beginning with God; all things were made through him, and without him was not anything made that was made" (Jn 1:1-3).

There is some similarity between God and the people he created. "God created man in his own image" (Gen 1:27). We have personalities like God. We are creative like he is. We think. We choose. But in no sense are we identical to God. As the book of Isaiah puts what is found elsewhere in the Bible so frequently, "Thus says the LORD, . . . I am the LORD, and there is no other" (Is 45:18-19).

Indeed there are ways in which we are very much unlike God. He is infinite. We are finite. He has also totally rejected anything evil. As the prophet Habakkuk put it, "Thou ... art of purer eyes than to behold evil and canst not look on wrong" (Hab 1:13). We, on the other hand, have not only looked on evil, we've done it. In Paul's letter to the Romans, he writes, "All have sinned and fall short of the glory of God" (Rom 3:23). All we need do is look around us (and in us) to see this is so. Murder. Corruption. Poverty. Crime. War. As G. K. Chesterton said, the Fall is the only doctrine that can be proven empirically.

Yet est holds that the world is perfect just the way it is. Erhard states, "Sometimes people get the notion that the purpose of est is to make you better. It is not. I happen to think you are perfect just the way you are."[57] In essence, everyone is saved already.

Jesus, in contrast, denied we are perfect already. Change is needed. "Unless you repent you will all likewise perish," he said (Lk 13:3). The beginning of salvation is first recognizing one's own need to change. Second is understanding that the ability to change is not to be found within oneself but within God—the opposite of est's view which finds the source of everything in oneself. If we are to get back into a right relationship with the Creator of the universe and begin therefore to live in harmony with his universe, we must go through Christ himself. "I am the way, the truth, and the life," Jesus told his disciples; "no one comes to the Father, but by me" (Jn 14:6).

Since we cannot repay God adequately for the damage we have done to ourselves, to others or to his world, we must rely on Jesus' death on the cross as sufficient repayment and accept as a free gift God's offer of new life. This means giving up our own attempts to control life and turning ourselves over to God rather than, as est suggests, accepting the fact that we are already in control.

Out of gratitude to God for making us whole, out of the love which he instills in us when he gives new life, out of obedience to a sovereign Lord, comes the Christian commitment to offer healing and reconciliation and peace to the world. Correcting the evils and injustices of the world is a prime concern of every believer.

In contrast, est fosters an apathy toward the world, a lack of care and compassion. If "what is, is," and is because we have chosen it to be that way, why change? One graduate, Dale, tells about what happened to a friend after he took est: "He had a 'so what' attitude and flunked out of school after his second quarter. Est teaches you that if you have problems, you've chosen to have them. My friend must have thought that he had chosen to have problems at U.C. . . . But he never had any before he took est."[58]

Apathy is also seen in some of the special vocabulary of est. To "assist" is good. To "help" is bad since it is believed to take away another's responsibility. To assist people is to lend support, recognizing that if one gave them no support, they could still get along quite well. To help someone is "an admission that he or she is incapable of accomplishing the act alone. According to est, helping should be avoided."[59]

This philosophy of life is taken to morbid extremes in est. Peter Marin reports, "I listened for two hours in [an est] graduate seminar to two women therapists explaining to me how we are all entirely responsible for our destinies, and how the Jews must have wanted to be burned by the Germans, and that those who starve in the Sabel must want it to happen, and when I ask them whether there is anything we owe to others, say, to a child starving in the desert, one of them snaps at me angrily: 'What can I do if a child is determined to starve?' "[60]

Why then does est sponsor the Hunger Project? In December 1978 *Mother Jones* magazine ran an article by Suzanne Gordon entitled "Let Them Eat est" to answer just that question. Actress Valerie Harper, an est supporter, said those who enroll in the Hunger Project (of which there are about two million) will create "a critical mass of agreement about an idea, and then out of that, things will manifest." That is, if we all align our thinking on the hunger issue, if an agreement is reached, a "context will be created in which hunger cannot exist" and starvation will somehow end.

Sending money to food relief organizations is considered by the Hunger Project to be a dehumanizing act. So almost none of the $8 million has gone to actually help the hungry. Instead, the money is used to tell more people about the Hunger Project. Est's own literature says it goes "to support the public educational endeavors of this organization."[61] Lester Brown, an authority in the field of world food problems, says that the Hunger Project has "probably collected more money in the name of hunger and done the least about hunger than any group I can think of." *Mother Jones* says the project is "a thinly veiled recruitment arm for est."

All of this is consistent with est's philosophy. If it exists (hunger, war, divorce or whatever), it must be right and good since I created it and I am God. But one could create something like the Hunger Project as a game to play in our universe. To escape boredom, I must arbitrarily choose for some things to be more important than others.[62] All this is similar to the Hindu notion of divine play *(lila)*. In any case we must never help, only assist.

So What?

The est graduation booklet states, "Obviously the truth is what's so. Not as obviously, it's also 'so what?' " Erhard and his est graduates say "so what?" to evil, greed, hate and suffering in the world. "So est is evil, what's the point? Yeah, I got that, now what? So what?"[63] Werner plays his game as God telling us of our divinity while millions starve to death. He preaches a belief that robs people of their values, morals and dignity in the name of enlightenment. How appropriate are the words of Isaiah: "Woe to those who call evil good and good evil, who put darkness for light and light for darkness, who put bitter for sweet and sweet for bitter! Woe to those who are wise in their own eyes, and shrewd in their own sight!" (Is 5:20-21).

6

Hare Krishna (ISKCON)

J. Isamu Yamamoto

*The Blessed Lord said: "The yogi whose mind
is fixed on Me verily attains the highest happiness.
A true yogi observes Me in all beings and also
sees every being in Me. Indeed, the self-realized man
sees Me everywhere. And of all yogis, he
who always abides in Me with great faith, worshiping
Me in transcendental loving service, is most
intimately united with Me in yoga and is the
highest of all."*
Bhagavad-Gita[1]

EACH SUMMER SINCE 1967 DEVOTEES of Krishna parade through Golden Gate Park in San Francisco. The grand event is known as the "Festival of the Chariots" or the *Ratha-yatra*, and the devotees celebrate Krishna in his deity form as Jagannatha, the Lord of the Universe. In this parade three enormous carts are pulled and pushed by Krishna devotees. Each cart enshrines a deity and contains idols and images. The other devotees, dressed in saffron robes, dance and chant around the carts. The male devotees are further distinguished by their *sikha* (shaved heads and pigtails).

If this scene of Krishna devotees chanting and dancing in the streets elicits any response from us, it should be more than a casual glance and a judgmental thought. We need to look beyond the unusual spectacle and understand why people are desperately seeking escape from this materialistic world and from their own sin and suffering, and why they are seeking truth in this way. Instead of scorning these devotees of Krishna, we should attempt to understand their doctrines and religious practices, for only by understanding may we be sensitive to their needs and thereby share the good news of Jesus Christ.

Background

In the Hindu pantheon of India there emerged three significant gods with variant characteristics. Brahma, Shiva and Vishnu represent the divine functions of creation, destruction and preservation respectively. These three personal deities are the manifestations of Absolute Reality, or what is known in Hindu doctrine as the *trimurti* of Brahman-Atman.

Vishnu is one of the most popular deities in India. He "is said to be the primal person and the first-born of creation, who has neither beginning nor end. In fact, Vishnu appears to be regarded by his devotees as the sole source of the universe, active in all three of its phases: creation, preservation and dissolution."[2]

Despite his many attributes, Vishnu's primary function is illuminated by his own name, which means "pervader." As preserver and protector of the universe, his most important feature exists in his avatars *(avataras)* or incarnations "into animal or human form in order to redress the balance of good and evil in the world by supporting the forces of good. . . . Today it is common to list ten famous *avataras* as the foundation of an evolutionary Vaisnavite theology."[3] This list includes Matsya, the Fish; Kurma, the Tortoise; Varaha, the Boar; Vamana, the Dwarf; Narasimha, the Man-Lion; Parašurama, Rama, Krishna and Buddha, men with various attributes; and Kalkin, the avatar to come. Although the meaning of avatar remains the same, not all lists of avatars are identical. Nevertheless, no list would exclude Krishna, the eighth avatar, for of all the avatars he is the best-loved and the most enchanting.

Adoration for Krishna grew through the centuries to the point that his importance overshadowed that of Vishnu in the eyes of many Hindus. One such Hindu was Sri Krishna Caitanya Mahaprabhu, a Bengalese Brahmin born in 1486 and founder of the Krishnaite sect. After being spiritually initiated as a *sannyasi* (one who has renounced the world) of the Bharati Order, Caitanya became a dynamic advocate of Vishnuism and particularly of Krishnaism.

Since he was an exponent of *bhakti* (the way of devotion), Caitanya danced and chanted the name of Krishna in the streets. This direct love of Krishna, he taught, was the surest way to burn off ignorance and karma (the consequences of past actions) and attain bliss. Because he worshiped exclusively by chanting, singing and dancing, however, orthodox Brahmins reproved him for being frivolous. Nevertheless, his argumentative brilliance and personal charisma attracted many followers who worshiped him as the incarnation of Krishna. Caitanya's sect of Krishnaism flourished in Bengal and the northeast of India.

Almost four hundred years later, a Vishnuite sannyasi, Sri Srimad Bhaktisiddhanta Sarasvati Gosvami Maharaja, initiated Prabhupada (born Abhay Charan in Calcutta on September 1, 1896) into the Gaudiya Vaishnava Society, heritors of Caitanya's sect of Vishnuite Hinduism. Charan had already graduated from the University of Calcutta in 1920, with majors in philosophy, economics and English.[4] In his thirties, he encountered Bhaktisiddhanta who, shortly before he died in 1936, commissioned Prabhupada to spread the teachings of Caitanya in English to the West.

In 1944, Charan attempted to express his religious ideas in English in the magazine *Back to Godhead*. His work with this periodical was highly successful and he was given the title *Bhaktivedanta*, "devotional knowledge."

In the laws of Manu (a system based on duty and not on coercion), an Indian man is to pass through four stages of life *(asramas)*. A man's first stage is as a celibate student *(Brahmacari)*; second stage, as a householder *(Grhastha)*; and third stage, as one who retires into the forest with his wife if he has one *(vanapratha)*. In his fourth stage he is a *sannyasi,* a person who renounces the worldly life. At the age of fifty-eight, Charan left his wife and five children.

He left his prosperous pharmaceutical business and donned the saffron robes of a Hindu monk. He then assumed the title of *swami* (a Hindu religious leader).

At the age of seventy Charan came to the United States to fulfill the commission of his deceased master that he spread the teachings of Krishna consciousness throughout the Western world. On September 18, 1965, he arrived in New York City, where he seated himself beneath a tree in Tomkins Park in the Lower East Side and commenced to chant the names of Krishna to the rhythm of his cymbals. The following year he established a temple in New York City, and soon temples appeared in other cities. By 1968 he had restarted *Back to Godhead* in the United States, and his young followers honored him with the name *Prabhupada*, which means "at whose feet masters sit."

Abhay Charan De Bhaktivedanta Swami Prabhupada had brought an exotic Indian religion to the West. It is known as the International Society for Krishna Consciousness (ISKCON), or simply the Krishna-consciousness movement. In a dozen years he published some seventy volumes of translation and commentary on India's holy scriptures and organized his international society into a worldwide confederation of *ashramas*, schools, temples and farm communities. He died November 14, 1977, in India's Vrndavana.

As early as 1970, Prabhupada had created a Governing Body Commission, which now consists of twenty-four senior devotees, all personally selected by him to supervise ISKCON's missionary activities in various zones around the world. Prabhupada did not pick a single disciple to succeed him as leader, as is customary in Hindu tradition. Instead, his disciples carry forward his movement with eleven senior disciples who act as initiating gurus to continue the movement's growth.

The Hare Krishna Movement Today
The impact of the Krishna movement in the United States has been slight in numbers. Although there are no exact statistics concern-

ing the number of adherents, ISKCON "claimed 68 centers and about 3,000 followers spread in the U.S.A. by 1972."[5] By the time of his death in 1977, Prabhupada had built a movement that had 10,000 full-time monks.[6]

Nevertheless, a flood of books, magazines and newspaper articles have been written about the Krishna devotees. They are visible in all our major cities. Prabhupada had said, "We will build a World Center for ISKCON in Manhattan among the skyscrapers, where people pass by every day, and it will be like a beacon."[7]

Officially the Hare Krishna movement supports itself through the manufacture and sale of incense, magazines and books (authored by Prabhupada). ISKCON leaders claim a monthly circulation of about 300,000 copies of *Back to Godhead*.[8] Furthermore, they say that their annual income from the sale of books is $16 million. In addition to their commercial enterprises, the devotees solicit funds for their movement to maintain their ISKCON centers.

It is also known that at least a few donors have contributed substantially to the Hare Krishna movement. Ex-Beatle George Harrison has composed and cut songs in dedication to Krishna. He has given funds from his royalties and his concerts to the movement. Alfred Ford, a great-grandson of the founder of the Ford Motor Company, has supported the movement. Other contributors include prominent Indian businessmen and industrialists.

The Spiritual Master

Swami Prabhupada, the guiding spirit of the Hare Krishna movement, was a Sanskrit scholar who translated, interpreted and presented the ancient literature of India to the West. His disciples receive his work with utmost reverence: "Bhaktivedanta [Prabhupada] is the ultimate standard of Krishna consciousness.... They must give him the honor due to God, because the guru is the transparent *via media* or representative of God and is distributing unalloyed love of God."[9]

Krishna devotees consider Prabhupada to be higher than Christ, located in the divine hierarchy above Brahma and Shiva, and below only Vishnu. Bali Mardan Maharaj, president of the New York ISKCON center, says, "Prabhupada was a world-genius, greater than Jesus."[10] "Only the spiritual master, Prabhupada, is ever referred to as His Divine Grace."[11]

Prabhupada's divine status has more than abstract or devotional significance. On a very practical level, he is believed to have the powers and prerogatives of a god. For example, he has the ability to take the "bad karma" of a devotee upon himself. What he does with it then is presumably between Krishna and himself, but in any case he is believed to deal with it in a way that obviously places him in the role of mediator between God (Krishna) and disciple.

Doctrine and Beliefs

The Vedantic version of Hinduism, which seeks to experience union with an impersonal Absolute (the "one" or Brahman), is commonly encountered in the West. The devotees of Krishna make it very plain that they differ from the monistic philosophy of Vedanta, basing their beliefs instead on the theistic strain of Vedantic philosophy. Krishnaites consider Brahma, Vishnu and Shiva to be expansions or forms of Krishna, who is the Supreme Personality, the Lord, the complete whole and the Absolute Truth.

Because Brahman (the impersonal Absolute) has only 78 per cent of Krishna's attributes, to try to merge oneself with Brahman, as the monistic Vedantists do, is to seek only eternity and knowledge while missing the absolute pleasure which is in Krishna. Rather than a final merging into the Absolute, therefore, the followers of Krishna look toward a transcendental love and fellowship with a personal deity, Krishna, who dwells in the heart of every person.

Although the movement itself has numerous commentaries on Vedic scriptures and has established a religious system of discipline and thought from them, it teaches its devotees to avoid mundane or philosophical speculation. Salvation for Krishna devotees is having a personal relationship with their god Krishna, and that salvation is attained through purification by complete surrender in devotion to Krishna. Furthermore, as Krishna consciousness deepens, the devotee will experience an increasing transcendental spiritual pleasure surpassing any found in the false world of materiality. As Christ is to Christians, Krishna is to Krishna devotees. Krishna is their personal savior.

Although Krishna appears little in the *Vedas* and the *Upanishads* (*shrutis*, "heard teachings"), he plays a significant role in later Hindu scriptures (*smrtis*, "remembered teachings"). In the famous epic *Bhagavad-Gita*, Krishna is Arjuna's charioteer and teacher. In the *Mahabharata*, Krishna is the heroic god and chief among warriors. In the *Puranos*, there are numerous myths about Krishna: as a child, Krishna is loved by parents; as a youth, Krishna is loved as a dear friend; as a lover, Krishna is loved as a lover. These stories which the *Puranas* tell about Krishna are depictions of people's devotion to Krishna. He is the conqueror of human hearts.

Devotees of Krishna accept the Puranic stories of the appearance of Krishna as historical fact. They believe that Krishna, in a human shape (though not as a human being), walked the earth five thousand years ago in the Indian forest of Vrindaban, where he danced with a hundred milkmaids at one time, all of them lost in orgiastic bliss and each convinced that he was making love to her alone. Each milkmaid had stolen out into the dangerous forest during the middle of the night at the risk of social disapproval to have a love affair with Krishna. This kind of love will risk everything for Krishna.

In this Puranic myth, Krishna favored the girl Radha, with whom he had a long affair and who became his consort. The experience of loving union and the experience of separation between Krishna and Radha reflect the love which devotees have for Krishna and symbolize the divine-human relationship which is the heart of the Krishnaite religion.

Spiritual Practice
Chanting is one of the most important rituals of the ISKCON lit-

urgy. It is also the aspect of the Krishna movement which is best known to the outside world. It is from this practice in fact that the group has received its popular name—"Hare Krishna." According to the Krishna-consciousness movement, the Vedic scriptures recommend constant chanting of the name of God for the purpose of developing love of Krishna and to attain salvation through union with him.

That which is chanted is the *mantra*, and the mantra is the code and signal by which to remember, picture and experience all that has been learned in connection with the absolute. The mantra consists of the Sanskrit words *Hare Krishna, Hare Krishna, Krishna Krishna, Hare Hare, Hare Rama, Hare Rama, Rama Rama, Hare Hare*. This formula is sung to the musical accompaniment of drums and harmonium. Each devotee is expected to chant at least sixteen rounds each day—a "round" consists of singing the mantra once on each of 108 prayer beads.

The chanting of this ancient formula is, of course, an invocation of specific Hindu deities and therefore has obvious spiritual implications. Although the books of the Hare Krishna movement strongly teach that a devotee should not stop thinking and become impersonal, but should concentrate on the Supreme Personality of Godhead, the chanting does resemble the mystical practices of impersonalist, monistic Hinduism. "The common element is the elimination of consciously directed thought so as to alter consciousness. Whether the object of meditation is one's own breathing, ... the intricate visual symbol of the *mandala*, ... or the repeated sound of the *mantra*, senses and thought are suspended. The *mantra* is repeated ... until awareness of the external world is shut out. The *mantra* is then continued to eliminate all thought."[12]

Faye Levine comments: "Having thus begun, I saw that chanting was crucial to the Hare Krishna's state of mind. For starters, it regularized the breathing, drove out all other thoughts, helped you forget yourself, made you feel a part of the group, and filled up your head with itself."[13]

Another significant feature of the Hare Krishna practice is their regular temple ceremonies. The most important of these relate to worshiping and attending to the "needs" of several deity-statues. These idols are presented with food, incense, flowers, a fan, a handkerchief and an offering of flames. During the ceremony, the deities are symbolically dressed and bathed, and at night they are "put to bed." While it is believed that Krishna is able to incarnate into a figure of wood, stone or metal which has been formed according to authorized instructions, it is also taught that the statues are not idols in the proper sense of the word, since Krishna only appears on earth in spiritual form.

Another important ceremony (repeated twice daily) involves the worship of a *Tulasi* bush (Indian basil shrub). The bush, which is thought to be of divine origin, is first placed upon a velvet-covered altar. Then the devotees bow to it, touching their foreheads to the floor. After presenting the bush with offerings of flowers and incense, they dance and chant around it for half an hour.

Common Ground for Witnessing

In sharing the good news of Jesus Christ with devotees of Krishna, we need not be scholars, but we do need to understand their beliefs and practices. It is a sad commentary on Christians when we followers of Christ look upon Krishna devotees with ridicule and derision, remarking how weird and strange they are. This is tragic in view of Christ's admonition that we are to be light to a dark world, salt to a starved people and love to crying hearts. David prayed, "Create in me a clean heart, O God. . . . Then I will teach transgressors thy ways, and sinners will return to thee. . . . The sacrifice acceptable to God is a broken spirit; a broken and contrite heart, O God, thou wilt not despise" (Ps 51:10, 13, 17).

John Stott says, "True dialogue is a mark of *integrity*. For in the conversation we listen to our friend's real beliefs and problems, and divest our minds of the false images we may have harboured."[14] Before we discuss with Hare Krishna devotees the differences between the two faiths, we need to realize what common ground Christians have with them. To know the similarities will be of benefit in two ways. First, a smoother line of communication will be set up, person to person, between Christian and devotee. Defensiveness will be relaxed, arguments can be avoided and trust will develop. Second, deeper insight into the differences between Krishna and Christ will invariably arise. Often by not taking the time and energy to find points of agreement with others, we miss the true difference in our positions. Instead we debate fruitlessly for hours on abstract concepts or trivial ideas like two people talking on the telephone with the line cut.

Christians and Krishna devotees share an obvious but important similarity: both are absorbed in a belief system. Both believe in a god, though it may not be the same one. We should understand that Krishna devotees, like Christians, believe that inherent in people is the need to be fulfilled by a higher being—a Supreme Being, if you will. This common yearning can be a strong, initial link for sharing.

Perhaps the most important common ground is that Christians and devotees alike believe in a god and savior who is personal. Unlike many Hindu monists, Krishna devotees recognize the need for a personal relationship with a deity-lord. Hence, we have two gods who can be compared and contrasted, rather than two religious philosophies to be debated. Furthermore, because the heart is significant in Christianity and Krishnaism, the needs of the human spirit can be more readily revealed and discussed.

Other points of agreement are complete devotion to a god, total commitment to a cause, the communion of believers, regular worship, and dedication to holy scriptures. Although the outward manifestations and the efficacy of the two faiths are distinctly different, these as well as other differences can be discussed once common ground is established.

Jesus, the Way

Krishna devotees revere Jesus and his teachings. The Bible is a source of spiritual inspiration and instruction for them. Nevertheless, their regard for Jesus is quite different from the orthodox position of Christianity. If there is any single question around which a Christian's dialog with a devotee should revolve, it is, Who is Jesus Christ and what has he done for us according to the Bible? The authority of Jesus as God and his death and resurrection as a man should be shared logically and gently, with the support of Scriptures and without diffidence.

Certainly some devotees will resist the authority of the Bible. But if they are honest with you and true to the teachings of their own leaders (who esteem the Bible as holy scripture), then the Bible will play a key role in establishing the credentials of Jesus Christ. The difficulty is readjusting their method of interpretation. This is why we, as Christians, must be grounded in the Word ourselves. We need not be biblical scholars nor have a degree from a seminary, but we should be ashamed if we, who have known and accepted the Lord Jesus, cannot share and explain his work according to the Word. "Do your best to present yourself to God as one approved, a workman who has no need to be ashamed, rightly handling the word of truth. . . . [You] must not be quarrelsome, but kindly to every one, an apt teacher, forbearing, correcting [your] opponents with gentleness. God may perhaps grant that they will repent and come to know the truth" (2 Tim 2:15, 24-25).

It is essential to establish that everyone is a sinner (Rom 3:9). Krishna devotees will usually not object to this. That is why Krishna is their lord and savior. But this point needs to be made, nonetheless, in order for you to testify to Christ as the sole redeemer (Heb 10:10). Once sin is understood, Christ and Krishna can be compared and contrasted.

Who is the savior? Can there be more than one savior? The Bible says, "Be it known to you all . . . that by the name of Jesus Christ of Nazareth, whom you crucified, whom God raised from the dead, by him this man is standing before you well. . . . And there is salvation in no one else, for there is no other name under heaven given among men by which we must be saved" (Acts 4:10, 12).

Furthermore, in Jesus Christ is the fullness of deity (Col 2:9). In the beginning he existed with God and as God (Jn 1:1). Even before the world existed, the Father and Christ shared a unique loving and personal relationship (Jn 17:24), of which anyone who believes in Jesus Christ and confesses him as Lord and Savior can be a part (Rom 5:10-11; 10:9-13).

Finally we must pray for those with whom we share Christ, for in prayer is the strength of our witness. Yet if we do pray for the deliverance and salvation of the followers of Krishna but do not share Christ with them, then surely our prayer will be as effective as a train without rails. According to French theologian Jacques Ellul, " 'Prayer requires that we do ourselves that which we ask God to do.' If I ask for us (and not for me!) our daily bread, I shall myself give this bread to those around me who lack it. If I pray for peace, I should undertake concretely to establish peace. . . . It teaches us quite rightly that prayer does not consist of words in thin air, and that a person cannot pray unless he is fully responsible for what he is saying."[15]

Let us not only pray for those in the world, such as the devotees of Krishna, who do not know our precious Lord Jesus, but let our hearts be broken for them so that we may love them personally on his behalf.

7

Jehovah's Witnesses

Wesley Walters
& Kurt Goedelman

*Reports are heard of brothers selling their
homes and property and planning to
finish out the rest of their days in this old system
in the pioneer service. Certainly this is a fine
way to spend the short time remaining
before the wicked world's end.*
Kingdom Ministry, 1974

A YOUNG MAN, TWENTY-TWO, was seriously injured in a car
accident in eastern Pennsylvania. Although he was suffering from
loss of blood, he refused a transfusion at the emergency room.
Lapsing into unconsciousness, he went into shock and died. He
was a Jehovah's Witness.

Who are these people who would rather die than receive a transfusion, who refuse to celebrate birthdays and Christmas, and who
announce specific dates for the destruction of the world and the
establishment of a new paradise on earth? What inspires such dedication?

Where They Came From
Although the Jehovah's Witnesses have been reticent about discussing their history, it is well established that their organization

was founded by Charles Taze Russell (1852-1916), son of a clothing merchandiser in Pittsburgh, Pennsylvania. In his early twenties Russell came under the influence of the Adventist movement begun by William Miller. Miller believed he had discovered from the Scriptures that Christ's second coming would occur in 1843, a date he subsequently changed to 1844.[1] When the event failed to take place, Miller simply admitted he had been mistaken. A number of Miller's followers, however, went back to their Bibles and worked out their own assorted date-setting systems.

Among these Adventists was N. H. Barbour of Rochester, New York, with whom Russell collaborated to publish in 1877 *Three Worlds and the Harvest of This World*.[2] The book set forth Barbour's view that Christ had returned invisibly in 1874 and that the dawn of a golden age could be expected in 1914. Charles Russell held this position the rest of his life. When he broke with Barbour over theological differences, he set forth his own views in *Zion's Watch Tower*, begun in 1879 and financed from the income of his clothing business. In 1884, blending his own teachings with some of Barbour's, he incorporated his group as the Watch Tower Bible and Tract Society.

During his life tenure as the first president of the Watchtower Society, Russell authored six volumes of the seven-volume series known as *The Studies in the Scriptures*. Although Russell never had any formal theological training, these works of his nevertheless provided the basis for the early theology that was adopted by the Watchtower followers. We know how important the series was to Russell from his claim that people would "go into darkness" by studying the Bible alone, without the aid of his *Studies*.[3]

In the *Studies* Russell regarded the Great Pyramid of Egypt as a prophecy in stone. By correlating historical events with the length of the corridors, Russell confirmed his 1874 date for the beginning of the tribulation which would precede the millennium, for the corridor ended in a pit at that point. Years after Russell's death the organization abandoned the 1874 date for a 1914 date. To accommodate the change, a new edition of *The Studies* (1923) simply added forty-one inches to the corridor's length in order to locate the *starting* point for the final years of earth's existence in 1914 or 1915.[4]

Russell's leadership lasted until his death in 1916. A few months after his death, the second president, Joseph F. Rutherford, came to power. Rutherford was even more prolific than Russell in producing books, issuing about a book a year. Over 300 million copies of his works were distributed during his presidency.

But he differed considerably from Russell in many of his biblical interpretations and consequently introduced a number of doctrinal changes. His replacement of Russell's teachings with his own, however, caused splinter groups to break off from the Watchtower. (Some of these, such as the Dawn Bible Students and the Layman's Home Missionary Movement, still exist.) Like Russell, Rutherford reached the point of unquestioned authority. In 1931 he bestowed upon the organization its present name of "Jehovah's Witnesses." It was Rutherford who initiated the door-to-door visitation program.

With the death of Rutherford in 1942, the 115,000 members of Jehovah's Witnesses took on new form and growth under their third president, Nathan H. Knorr. Knorr refined the organizational structure with many businesslike procedures and established training schools for Witnesses. His saleslike methods proved to be most effective, and the Society grew in both wealth and membership, claiming over two million members upon his death in 1977.

During Knorr's presidency Frederick W. Franz served as the vice president of the sect; upon Knorr's death he took control. Franz had been a key figure in Witness history even during Knorr's presidency. While Knorr concentrated his efforts on increasing the membership, Franz shaped current Witness theology.

Franz is upheld by the Society as its most knowledgeable Hebrew scholar. However, to keep this image he had to misrepresent himself under oath in a 1954 court trial in Scotland. After claiming a working knowledge of Hebrew, he was discredited when he could not cast a simple Bible verse (Genesis 2:4) back into Hebrew.[5]

Franz brought the organization through one of its most trying times—the failure of its prediction that the world would end in 1975. Some members, fully believing the Society's chronology, had sold their homes and property to devote themselves to full-time door-to-door service. Their in-house organ, *Kingdom Ministry*, had commended this act of dedication as an excellent way to spend the few remaining months before the world's end in 1975:

> Reports are heard of brothers selling their homes and property and planning to finish out the rest of their days in this old system in the pioneer service. Certainly this is a fine way to spend the short time remaining before the wicked world's end.[6]

Since 1980 Franz has also had to struggle to hold the organization together in the face of the disfellowshiping at Bethel Headquarters of several top leaders who had major doctrinal differences with Watchtower teachings. President Franz's own nephew, Raymond Franz, was removed from the Board of Directors and subsequently disfellowshiped. The Watchtower is built upon a shaky theological foundation, and lovers of truth who examine it carefully and discover its major cracks soon find themselves in deep trouble with the leadership.

What They Publish

The Watchtower Bible and Tract Society reportedly publishes more material than all other cultic groups in the world combined. The printed page is the major tool of Jehovah's Witnesses. Besides keeping present members in line with the current thought of the Society, their magazines and booklets make new converts.

Russell's initial printings of the *Watchtower* magazine in 1879 consisted of 6,000 copies per month. Today that figure has increased astronomically. The present *Watchtower* is bimonthly and has a total monthly printing of over 18 million copies released in 106 languages. The society's bimonthly *Awake!* (aimed at non-members) is printed in 40 languages with over 16 million copies per month.

On the average at least two new books also come off the Watch-tower presses each year, with the minimum printing being one million copies. Their introductory Bible study booklet, *The Truth That Leads to Eternal Life,* released in 115 languages, has become the third most published book of all time.

Jehovah's Witnesses have over the years cited more than seventy translations of the Bible in their effort to justify peculiar points in their theology. However, because the Bible does not in general support their thinking and because it is difficult to cite consistently from various versions, the Society under the direction of Knorr finally produced its own translation. In 1961 their work was completed, and a one-volume edition of *The New World Translation of the Holy Scriptures* was released.

This *New World Translation* is the product of a five-man translation committee, none of whom had adequate schooling in biblical languages.[7] Examination shows that the purpose of this work is not to present a modern translation, as claimed, but to provide a basis and support for Witness theology. For example, the Jehovah's Witnesses have consistently tried to eliminate from the Bible Jesus' claim to deity. A significant text dealing with this crucial biblical truth is John 1:1, which states that "the Word [Jesus] was God." The Society in its translation, however, has rendered this passage "and the Word was a god." Its translating *theos* as "a god" comes directly out of the anti-Trinitarian theology Witnesses bring to the Bible, rather than from the rules of Greek grammar as the Society claims. To justify its rendering, the Watch-tower has used the publications of a spiritist, a Christadelphian and the Unitarians. Similar alterations of the Scriptures can be found in Philippians 2:9 and Colossians 1:16-17, where words are again added to the text in order to change the clear meaning of Paul's statements. By these additions God's Son is reduced to one among many of God's created beings.

How They Respond to Biblical Teachings

Professor Edmund C. Gruss, formerly a Watchtower member,

speaks of the Jehovah's Witnesses as "apostles of denial." The Witnesses deny all major teachings of biblical Christianity: the Trinity, the personage of the Holy Spirit and, as we just noted, the deity of our Lord Jesus. Further, they disavow Jesus' bodily resurrection and his visible second coming. The Watchtower also denies the existence both of hell and of a heavenly home for all believers. For them salvation, the gift of eternal life to an otherwise mortal soul, is based not on Christ's death but on loyalty to Witness leaders: "Your attitude toward the wheatlike anointed 'brothers' of Christ . . . will be the determining factor as to whether you go into 'everlasting cutting-off' or receive 'everlasting life,' " warns the August 1, 1981, *Watchtower*.

Denying the Trinity. The Watchtower not only rejects the Trinity but ridicules this biblical truth, stating, "Sincere persons who want to know the true God and serve Him find it a bit difficult to love and worship a complicated freakish-looking three headed God. . . . The obvious conclusion is that Satan is the originator of the Trinity doctrine."[8]

In an effort to denounce the Trinity, the Watchtower has many times misstated the Christian position to make it appear that believers in the Triune God believe in not one but three Gods. This, however, is a perversion of biblical faith.

The doctrine of the Trinity emerges from the New Testament in several places. For example, it is clear in Scripture that each person of the Trinity is eternal (Ps 93:2; Mic 5:2; Heb 9:14), that each has shared in creation (Ps 100:3; Jn 1:3; Gen 1:2), that each has inspired Scripture (2 Tim 3:16; 1 Pet 1:10-11; 2 Pet 1:21) and, most important, that each is called God (Jn 6:27; Jn 20:28; Acts 5:3-4).

The Witnesses condemn Trinitarians as being in opposition to the Bible, but we need only a brief look at their theology to find that they are the ones opposing the biblical teaching. The Witnesses are virtually polytheists, having two true Gods who are completely separate beings, Jehovah the Almighty God and Jesus the mighty god through whom God made all things. But Scripture affirms that there is only one true God, and that distinguishable within that One is a complexity, a threeness. This is clear in Matthew 28:19, where the baptismal formula instituted by Jesus involves the one name (singular) of the three, Father, Son and Holy Spirit.

Denying the personality of the Holy Spirit. In their denial of the Trinity, Witnesses also deny the personality of the Holy Spirit. They claim that "the holy spirit is the invisible active force of Almighty God which moves his servants to do his will."[9] To a Witness, the Spirit is a mere impersonal force similar to electricity.

An examination of Scripture, however, reveals that the Spirit is more than an impersonal force. Personal traits are applied to him. In Romans 8:27 we see that the Spirit has a mind; in 1 Corinthians 12:11 that he possesses a will; in Romans 8:14 that he acts as a guide; in Acts 5:3-4 that he can be lied to; in Romans 8:26 that he intercedes for believers; and in Acts 13:2, along with Hebrews 3:7 and Revelation 2:7, that he can speak out directly. The Holy Spirit of the Bible is a person.

Denying the deity of Christ. Witnesses have announced that Jesus "was not Jehovah God, but was existing in God's form."[10]

Now the foundation of Christian faith, as expressly stated in Scripture, is in the person and work of our Lord Jesus Christ (Rom 10:9-10). The Bible is clear that Jesus is indeed God manifested in the flesh, as is evident from John 8:58 (compared to Exodus 3:14), John 20:28, Hebrews 1:8, Matthew 1:23 and Colossians 2:9. Furthermore, Matthew 4:10 affirms that only Jehovah God is to be worshiped; yet Jesus received and welcomed such worship repeatedly (see Mt 8:2; 9:18; 14:33; 15:25 and 28:9, 17), and the Father even commanded the angels to worship him (Heb 1:6).

Scripture teaches that Jesus created all things (Jn 1:3; Col 1:16-17). Yet Isaiah 44:24 states that *Jehovah alone* created the world. Clearly these two are One. That Jesus is God is the clear testimony of the Bible.

Denying Jesus' bodily resurrection. The basis of our hope as Christians is in the resurrection of our Lord, and the Witnesses too proclaim belief in his rising from the dead. But their claim is misleading since they really believe that he was resurrected merely

109

as a spirit. The Watchtower has announced that the body that died on the cross was either dissolved into gases or preserved in heaven as a memorial.[11] "The King Christ Jesus was put to death in the flesh and was resurrected an invisible spirit creature."[12] They maintain that this spirit of Jesus was able to materialize into bodies to prove his spiritual resurrection to his followers.[13]

Their view is therefore no better than that claimed by any other world religion whose leader's body never came back from the grave. The Watchtower Society in denying the bodily resurrection leaves its followers without hope, for the Bible, speaking of the bodily resurrection, declares that "if Christ has not been raised, your faith is futile and you are still in your sins" (1 Cor 15:17).

The Bible is most clear that Jesus' resurrection was a bodily one. Jesus himself stated in John 2:19-21 that his body would be raised and that he himself would raise it. This one passage alone establishes that his resurrection was physical, since the same temple (body) that his enemies would destroy is the one he promised to raise up. John's Gospel presents further evidence in that Thomas would not believe that Christ had come forth from the grave unless he saw and touched his crucifixion wounds—wounds which a newly materialized body would not bear (Jn 20:20-29).

The disciples once, like the Witnesses, made the mistake of regarding the resurrected Christ as only a spirit-being. Luke 24:37 explains that when Jesus appeared they supposed they were seeing a spirit. But Jesus calmed their fears by showing them his hands and feet, announcing that "a spirit has not flesh and bones as you see that I have" (v. 39).

The apostle Paul taught that Christ, now in heaven, still possesses a body, for he wrote concerning Christ that "in him the whole fulness of the deity *dwells bodily*" (Col 2:9). Writing twenty or more years after the crucifixion, Paul uses the present tense of "dwell," meaning that deity "is dwelling," even now, bodily in Jesus.

Denying the visible return of Jesus. The Watchtower's spiritual resurrection of Jesus makes possible its doctrine of his invisible second coming. For example, the Witnesses claim that "it is a settled Scriptural truth ... that human eyes will not see him at his second coming, neither will he come in a fleshly body."[14]

With this line of thinking implanted in the minds of Witnesses, it was easy for the Watchtower to proclaim that Christ had already returned invisibly. As late as 1929 the Society was still saying that the second coming had taken place in 1874.[15] The date now held to mark Christ's return is 1914. According to a recent *Watchtower*, "millions of persons around the world have come to recognize Christ's presence since the eventful year 1914."[16] Such confusion and revision of dates is only possible by positing Christ's invisibility.

Nowhere within the pages of Scripture, however, do we find Christ's second coming spoken of as being mysterious or hidden. In fact, Christ himself tells us in Matthew 24:23-27 that those who would claim his second coming to be hidden are false prophets. The blessed hope for believers is the "glorious appearing of our great God and Savior, Jesus Christ" (Tit 2:13 NIV). This return will truly be an open event when "every eye shall see him."

Denying immortality. Witnesses teach that the soul is merely a life force or principle which animates the body. Thus when the body dies, the soul also ceases to exist. Hence a person at death is similar to a beast, no different from a dead dog.[17]

This theology is vastly different from the teaching of passages like Philippians 1:21-24 and 2 Corinthians 5:6-8, which teach that death means being with the Lord.

The distorted view of human nature held by Witnesses also explains why there is for them no continuity to the person of Christ. In their view, Jesus pre-existed as the angel Michael. In becoming the human being Jesus, Michael simply ceased to exist. After Jesus' death, no part of him continued to exist either, and so God simply re-created him as a spirit-being again. In the Bible, however, it is the same person who persists through all phases of the Savior's existence.

Denying hell. The Watchtower's rejection of eternal punishment in hell is one of the leading attractions of Witness theology. Witness writers assert that hell is merely humanity's common grave and that the idea that it is a place of punishment "cannot be true."[18]

The Witnesses fail to note, however, that our Lord Jesus spoke more on the subject of hell than he did of heaven. Hell, Jesus said, was originally prepared for the devil and his angels (Mt 25:41), but people have joined Satan in his open rebellion against God and will share his punishment. Scriptures such as Matthew 13:42, 25:46 and 26:24 clearly indicate that hell is a real place of suffering.

Limiting heaven. The Watchtower's teaching concerning the kingdom of heaven limits residents there to 144,000 believers. Witnesses arrive at this figure through a misinterpretation of Revelation 7:4. Sadly, countless Witnesses have no hope of a heavenly kingdom where they will dwell in the presence of the living God. Instead most Witnesses believe they will spend eternity on earth, separated from God's loving presence. However, biblical passages, such as John 14:2-3, 1 Thessalonians 4:13-18, Luke 23:39-43 and 2 Corinthians 5:8, offer to all who trust their God and Savior Jesus the assurance of a dwelling place in God's presence.

Other distinctives. One practice of the Witnesses which sets them apart from orthodox Christians is their rejection of blood transfusions. They base this scruple on the erroneous idea that transfusions are forbidden by Genesis 9:4 and similar texts. What these verses actually prohibit, however, is *eating* flesh with the blood still in it. Because of their misunderstanding, some Witnesses and their dependent children have met a premature and often preventable death.

Witnesses hold numerous other distinctive beliefs. They reject the celebration of Christmas. They believe that Christ died on a torture stake rather than on the traditional cross. They do not celebrate birthdays or holidays, holding that participating in these is a form of creature worship. They reject human government, military service and flag saluting, holding that such things are idolatry. Many of these doctrines are used as tactics to involve people in discussions of little or no important theological value.

What Keeps Them Going?

How do people come to accept such twisting of the Scriptures? The Society's leaders gain hold upon their followers by repeatedly asserting that their interpretation of Scripture comes directly from Jehovah. They base this claim upon an erroneous use of Matthew 24:45-47. The parable is twisted into a "prophecy" that the Society is the "faithful and wise servant." This servant, through the *Watchtower*, feeds the members their "meat [spiritual food] in due season."[19]

Charles Russell, who introduced this idea, first taught that the servant consisted of all his loyal Watchtower followers.[20] In 1896, however, Russell's wife suggested that since "servant" is singular, it must refer to only one individual, namely, her husband. From that time until his death, Russell defended his wife's interpretation and published numerous letters from his followers that stated he was "that servant."[21]

For ten years after his death the Watchtower, including President Rutherford, continued to teach that the faithful servant was exclusively Russell.[22] Suddenly in 1927 Russell was dethroned, and the Watchtower taught that the Christian congregation itself (speaking through the Watchtower leaders) was now the faithful servant.[23] It further asserted that those who regarded Russell as "that servant" (the very position the Watchtower had advocated for thirty years) were guilty of promoting creature worship, a sectarian act most repulsive to Jehovah.

There is an irony in these changing explanations of the servant being first a class, then an individual (Russell) and then a class again. By this shift Witnesses have destroyed the possibility that they could be the faithful servant of Matthew 24:45. If the Society was at one time correct in regarding Russell as "that servant," then in rejecting him as such they have abandoned God's messenger and his message.[24] If, on the other hand, Russell was falsely set forth as "that servant," then the Society is guilty of having promoted the creature worship of a deceiver. Either way it can hardly be regarded as God's organization chosen to restore truth to the earth.[25]

A Call to Witnesses and Christians

How may Jehovah's Witnesses come to a personal relationship with the Lord? First of all, Witnesses need to experience genuine Christian concern and love. Christian opposition to the Watchtower Society is like the opposition of parents to the alcohol that is destroying their son. They want to free their son to enjoy real life. Witnesses who come to Christ depend heavily on such Christian support and fellowship as they are inevitably expelled from the Society that had sustained them.

Second, Witnesses need to look at Bible verses in their setting. Most of the Watchtower Bible quotations are examined out of context. Christians can help by pausing to look up verses cited by Witnesses and asking, "How does the setting lead to the meaning the Society has given the verse?" A woman who was a Witness for twenty-seven years began looking up Bible passages for the purpose of converting a relative to the Society. Seeing the passages in their setting for the first time, she was startled to discover that Jesus really is God. Today she is a radiant Christian.

It is important to use a recognized version of the Bible. The Society prints both the King James Version and the 1901 American Standard Version. Both Witnesses and evangelical Christians can use these two translations without worrying about the pre-interpreted passages of the *New World Translation*.

Third, Witnesses need frankly to face the overwhelming fact that the Society has no authority to direct people's lives. The Watchtower organization has repeatedly claimed to be God's prophet on earth today. For example, the April 1, 1972, *Watchtower* asks: "Does Jehovah have a prophet to warn them of dangers and to declare things to come?" It answers in the affirmative and adds that "this 'prophet' was not one man, but was a body of men and women. It was the small group of footstep followers of Jesus Christ, known at that time as International Bible Students. Today they are known as Jehovah's Christian witnesses."[26]

The Bible makes it clear that whoever claims to be Jehovah's prophet must be validated by having his predictions fulfilled; otherwise he is clearly marked as a false prophet (Deut 18: 20-22). The Watchtower Society fully agrees that to be a true prophet one's prophecies "must come to pass," whereas a "would-be prophet . . . could not have his prophecies come true," and "that alone is strong evidence that they are false prophets."[27] Especially is this true of "those in times past who predicted an 'end to the world,' even announcing a specific date. . . . Yet, nothing happened. The 'end' did not come. They were guilty of false prophesying," the Society declares.[28]

In light of the Watchtower's frequent statement of this principle, Witnesses may look openly at the Society's repeated failures in predicting the end of the world. Under Russell's leadership the Watchtower declared that the final battle (Armageddon or "the battle of the great day of God Almighty") "will end in A.D. 1914 with the complete overthrow of the earth's present rulership."[29] Later the Society set 1925 and then again 1975 as the end dates.[30] These failures have shown the Watchtower, by its own definitions, to be a false prophet.[31] The Witness who desires spiritual truth should abandon the Society as a dependable spiritual guide. Jehovah himself will guide those who turn to him for forgiveness and light (Ps 32:5-8).

Finally Witnesses and Christians need to give each other a fair hearing. Christians claim to have a living fellowship with the Lord like that promised in the Bible. Sin had separated humanity from God, but his love for them was so strong that he took human form so that he could suffer the penalty for them (Is 59:2; Rom 5:8). Christians have found that everlasting life is something they can have right now (Jn 3:36). They have learned that no amount of faithful service can earn them God's approval (Eph 2:8-10; Tit 3:5; Rom 3:23), although he expects good works of his people.

As Christians share with Witnesses their own experience of coming to the Lord, the invitation is extended to them. Since it is ultimately the Lord with whom each of us must relate, the Witness may call on him to show the truth about Jesus. Many Witnesses have found peace with God in Christ through such sincere pleadings with God. And, conversely, many Christians have been challenged by the zeal of Jehovah's Witnesses to be more faithful in serving the Triune God.

8

Latter-day Saints (Mormons)

Donald S. Tingle

*I say to the whole world, receive the truth,
no matter who presents it to you.*
Brigham Young, Journal of Discourses

THE MORMONS CLAIM TO BE the fastest-growing religious organization in the world, and their impressive statistics add weight to that claim. When they held their 151st Annual General Conference in April 1981, they had grown to almost 4,638,000 members in 83 countries. Thirty thousand missionaries continue to win more converts daily. In 1980, 578 converts were baptized daily, making a total of 211,000 for the year, not counting 65,000 baptisms of children who were raised Mormons.[1]

In 1981 the Mormons announced plans for constructing nine smaller temples, making a total of thirty-seven temples either built, under construction, or planned. Construction plans for seven temples were announced the year before.[2] In the past, visiting a temple could be a once-in-a-lifetime experience for some people, but now temples will be more accessible to the growing numbers of faithful Mormons.

When Joseph Smith and five other men organized this church on April 6, 1830, no one could have guessed it would reach the magnitude it has today. What is their history? What do they believe? Are they truly Christian? In what follows I will present not only Mormon answers to these questions but also some results of independent scholarship.

History of the Mormons

In the *History of the Church*, Mormon scholar B. H. Roberts argues that "the Church founded by the labors of Jesus and His Apostles was destroyed from the face of the earth" by the time of Constantine.[3] This is an important assumption for Mormons, because "nothing less than a complete apostasy from the Christian religion would warrant the establishment of the Church of Jesus Christ of Latter-day Saints" (LDS church).[4]

Jesus, by contrast, taught that the church would never be destroyed, that there would never be a complete apostasy, that "the gates of hell shall not prevail against it" (Mt 16:18). Corruption and satanic attacks are matters of record in church history, but the church of Christ has in fact prevailed. Even Roberts admits this, contrary to his previous argument, when he says, "Yet God left not Himself without witnesses in the earth; for there were a few in all dispensations who honored Him and His righteous laws."[5]

Joseph Smith himself, two years before his death, explained how he came to start this new church. According to his account, religious excitement swept through his part of New York State in 1820 when he was 14 years old. After several from his family joined the Presbyterian church, he seriously reflected upon which church to join. He said that "so great were the confusion and strife among the different denominations, that it was impossible ... to come to any certain conclusion who was right and who was wrong." One day he read James 1:5, "If any of you lack wisdom, let him ask of God, that giveth to all men liberally, and upbraideth not; and it shall be given him."

Choosing to ask God for guidance, Joseph retired to the woods in the spring of 1820 to pray. It was then that he received his "First Vision." He said he saw a pillar of light brighter than the sun. Then God the Father and Jesus Christ appeared in glorified bodily form. They commanded him not to join any of the religious groups, "for they were all wrong."[6]

On September 21, 1823, Joseph claimed to have received a visit from the angel Moroni who informed him of a book written upon golden plates hidden in a hill nearby. Glasses (the Urim and Thummim) were deposited with the plates to help with the translation. The plates recorded God's dealings with the former inhabitants of America. On September 22, 1827, the angel delivered the plates to Joseph to translate. These became the *Book of Mormon*, copyrighted on June 11, 1829. Five thousand copies were printed in Palmyra, New York, in 1830. Once the translation was completed, the plates were returned to the angel Moroni and are not now available for inspection. There is, therefore, no concrete evidence the plates ever existed.

Before the plates were taken from the earth, three witnesses prayed with Joseph that they might see them. An angel appeared and showed the plates individually so they could see the engravings on them. Their testimony about the plates is found in the front of the *Book of Mormon*. All three witnesses, Martin Harris, Oliver Cowdery and David Whitmer, left the LDS church. Harris came back in his old age, but Cowdery joined the Methodist church and before his death agreed with Whitmer that the LDS church was not God's true church. David Whitmer in *An Address to All Believers in Christ* (1887) claimed that Joseph Smith by 1833 had become a false prophet. However, he still maintained his testimony to the *Book of Mormon*.[7] Eight others later also claimed to have witnessed the plates.

According to Joseph Smith and Oliver Cowdery, on May 15, 1829, John the Baptist appeared to them saying, "Upon you ... I confer the priesthood of Aaron, which holds the keys of the ministering of angels, and of the gospel of repentance, and of baptism by immersion for the remission of sins." The Melchizedek Priesthood was supposedly received from Peter, James and John before June.[8]

Joseph Smith founded the "Church of Christ" on April 6, 1830 (the name was later changed to its current form, the Church of Jesus Christ of Latter-day Saints). At the founding meeting Joseph received a revelation that he was to be "a seer, a translator, a prophet, an apostle." His authority was attested shortly thereafter when he cast a demon from a man who had been "caught up off the floor and tossed about most fearfully."[9]

Sidney Rigdon, an Ohio minister who had recently left the Disciples of Christ, was publicly converted to the Mormon faith when Oliver Cowdery, Parley Pratt and others traveled west on a missionary journey. Pratt, also a former Disciple, gave Rigdon a copy of the *Book of Mormon*, and a short time later Rigdon and many of his congregation became converts. When the missionaries left in December, a thousand members reportedly had been added to the church in the Kirtland, Ohio, area. Rigdon himself served as Joseph Smith's right-hand man for many years.

Many other Mormons moved west to Kirtland where "the basic organization of Church government was established; many fundamental and distinguishing doctrines were pronounced by Joseph Smith."[10] Joseph began work on an "inspired" revision of the Bible. A "School of Prophets" was organized. And "A Word of Wisdom" was given, warning against the use of tobacco, alcoholic beverages, "hot drinks" and too much meat.[11] In Kirtland they dedicated their first temple on March 27, 1836.

Another settlement had been formed in Jackson County, Missouri, and when the church in Kirtland faced severe opposition, they joined those in Missouri. In Jackson County they planned to build Zion, an American Jerusalem where Indians and Mormon believers would be safe from destruction at the return of Christ which would occur by 1891. Joseph prophesied that they would build a great temple to God "in this generation" at the temple lot in Zion (Independence, Missouri).[12]

This prophecy remains unfulfilled, since in 1838-39 the Mormons fled to Illinois under the direction of Brigham Young. Joseph, temporarily detained in prison with the threat of death hanging over his head, later joined the faithful. They built from swampland along the Mississippi the beautiful city of Nauvoo. Converts from the eastern United States, Canada and the British Isles came to Nauvoo, and their ranks swelled to 20,000.

Trouble continued to break out between the Mormons and the Gentiles (non-Mormons). On June 24, 1844, Joseph and others set out for Carthage, where they had been summoned by the legal authorities. They were arrested and held in jail in Carthage. On June 27, a mob attacked the jail. Joseph sprang for his six-shooter, Hyrum (his brother) for his single-shot pistol, and the others for walking sticks. As the mob came up the stairs, Hyrum was shot dead. Joseph fired his six-shooter in the stairway. Seeing no safety in the room, and knowing the mob was after him primarily, he sprang to the window, was struck with three bullets and fell dead into the hands of his murderers.

The Mormons left their homes in Nauvoo, and under the direction of Brigham Young, who managed to seize control of the church, some of them made their treacherous journey to the Great Salt Lake in Utah, where they built a flourishing city. Others joined them later by wagon train, and some pulled handcarts.

The Reorganized Church of Jesus Christ of Latter-day Saints, with its headquarters in Independence, Missouri, was officially founded in 1860. It has been presided over by direct descendants of Joseph Smith since that time. On two occasions (1880 and 1894) civil courts ruled that the Reorganized Church has "been sustained as the successor of the original church presided over by the Martyr Joseph Smith."[13] Several basic doctrinal differences exist between the LDS and Reorganized churches. Moreover, there are nearly a hundred other Mormon sects. The analysis in this book concerns primarily the LDS church itself.

This history section has been written as most Mormons today know it; however, there are six versions of the First Vision, a dozen variations about finding and translating the plates, and several versions of the witnesses to the plates.[14] This raises serious questions about the validity of Joseph Smith's claims for his visions and teachings. Mormons should examine his claims not only by asking for wisdom from God in prayer but also by doing serious historical research. For a true testimony from God and historical facts never will contradict one another.

Authority and Structure
The "Standard Works of the Church" for the Mormons are fourfold: the Bible, *Book of Mormon, Doctrine and Covenants* and *Pearl of Great Price.* These constitute the written authority of the LDS church. In addition, since Mormons believe in continued revelation, new books approved by the President can be published by or for the church and be considered authoritative.

Every person in the church can receive private revelations, but only the President can speak with authoritative revelation for the entire church; he is "a seer, a revelator, a translator, and a prophet."[15] The President is assisted by two Counselors, these three forming the First Presidency. Below them are the Council of the Twelve (Apostles). Below them are the Presidency of the First Quorum of the Seventy (seven presidents) and additional members of the First Quorum. Below them are additional quorums throughout the world. The Presiding Bishopric (usually three members) is in charge of all activities pertaining to the Aaronic Priesthood. There is also a Presiding Patriarch who can bless, curse, bind and loose, for he holds the keys to the patriarchal office. Other patriarchs serve locally.

The church is divided into stakes presided over by stake presidencies; these are further divided into wards (local congregations) or branches, presided over by bishops. Presidents and bishops serve as pastors of the flock without pay (no paid ministry below the national level). There are also missions.

Members of the church progress up the ladder of work and authority if they are faithful and qualified. In the Aaronic Priesthood a man becomes (1) deacon, (2) teacher, (3) priest. Then he may be ordained to the Melchizedek Priesthood and become (4) elder, (5) seventies, (6) high priest, (7) patriarch and (8) apostle.

We may note here in passing that unmarried boys and young men are ordained deacons and elders without meeting the qualifications set down in the New Testament (see 1 Tim 3:1-13 and Tit 1:5-9). Neither do those ordained to the Aaronic Priesthood meet the qualification of being physical descendants of Aaron, despite the warning in Numbers 3:10: "And thou shalt appoint Aaron and his sons, and they shall wait on their priest's office: and the stranger that cometh nigh shall be put to death." According to the Bible, the Aaronic Priesthood was changed and replaced when Jesus became "a priest for ever after the order of Melchisedec." His qualification for that priestly honor was "the power of an endless life" which he had by virtue of his physical resurrection (Heb 7:16-17). No Mormon has shown his qualification to assume the Melchizedek priesthood by demonstrating the power of an endless life. Moreover, Jesus' priesthood is "unchangeable" (Heb 7:24), the original Greek word meaning "intransmissible," "without successors." We already have a faithful high priest who makes reconciliation for the sins of the people, Jesus Christ (Heb 2:17—3:1), and we have no need for any others. Also, all Christians (men and women) serve as priests under Jesus Christ (1 Pet 2:9-10).

At the time of their 151st anniversary, Mormons were dedicating about 1.5 church buildings per day throughout the world. In addition, Mormons also have temples. There a husband and wife can be sealed in marriage for time and eternity (contrary to Mt 22:30) In the temple all ordinances necessary for exaltation can be performed by proxy for dead ancestors, who in the spirit world can choose to accept or reject salvation. However, before these souls can be freed from their "prison house," someone must be baptized for those dead relatives to make possible their salvation (contrary to Alma 34:32-35 in the *Book of Mormon* and Heb 9:27). That is why they have the largest genealogical records on microfilm in the world.

The Bible. Article eight of the Mormon Articles of Faith states,

"We believe the Bible to be the word of God as far as it is translated correctly." James Talmage, Mormon Apostle, adds, "However, an impartial investigator has cause to wonder more at the paucity of errors than that mistakes are to be found at all."[16] Mormons believe that the original manuscripts of the Bible books were completely correct as God's Word, but they teach that errors have crept in through poor transmission of the texts and poor translations. With this argument they brush off key Scriptures which refute their doctrines, claiming that such passages are corrupt and in error.

This situation changed somewhat in 1979. That year the Corporation of the President copyrighted its own edition of the King James Version of the Bible which added numerous footnotes explaining whatever important corrections the LDS church felt should be noted from Joseph Smith's "inspired" translation.

Joseph Smith began this Bible revision in June of 1830, and most of it was completed by 1833, although some modifications continued to be made until his death in 1844. Joseph said on July 2, 1833, "We this day finished the translating of the scriptures."[17] Utah Mormons conjecture that "it is possible that some additional modifications would have been made had he lived to publish the entire work"[18] and have been reluctant to endorse the work as he left it. Joseph, however, testified that his translation was completed in fulfillment of his revelation to "continue the work of translation until it be finished."[19] The Reorganized Church publishes the entire translation today, but the LDS church has incorporated only excerpts from it into the notes of their KJV Bible.

Joseph Smith claimed to revise the Bible under the inspiration of God, not only rendering some passages differently but also adding sections. However, he revised his own translation over the years, sometimes changing a passage up to three times.[20] His revision has no basis whatever in the various Hebrew and Greek manuscripts available today; it cannot be verified by any objective evidence. These unfounded changes in the Bible, including several in the book of Revelation, are weighty evidence against Joseph

Smith when we read John's warning at the end of Revelation: "If any man shall add unto these things, God shall add unto him the plagues that are written in this book: And if any man shall take away from the words of the book of this prophecy, God shall take away his part out of the book of life, and out of the holy city, and from the things, which are written in this book" (Rev 22:18-19).

All Bible references in this chapter are from the KJV and have received no revision in any footnotes of the new Mormon Bible. So when such Scriptures contradict Mormon doctrine, Mormons should pay special attention. Joseph said that his translation of the Bible, which was done by the power of God, was completed. The President of the LDS church, who claims to be a prophet, approved which parts of the "Inspired Version" should be included in the footnotes. One would expect, therefore, that unrevised sections of the Bible should be accepted at face value by Mormons.

The Book of Mormon. Less than three years before his death, Joseph Smith said, "I told the brethren that the *Book of Mormon* was the most correct of any book upon the earth, and the keystone of our religion, and a man would get nearer to God by abiding by its precepts, than by any other book."[21] Nonetheless, since the 1830 edition of this "most correct" book, at least 3,913 changes have been made in the text, some relating to grammar and spelling and others to obvious distortions of the text.[22] The original handwritten manuscripts in the possession of both the Reorganized Church and the LDS church agree with the 1830 edition in several key sections that disagree with today's edition.[23] The Mormon Apostle James Talmage is responsible for many of the changes in the present edition of the *Book of Mormon,* and this was done without benefit of the Urim and Thummim.

The *Book of Mormon* tells the story of those who traveled to the Western Hemisphere from the Near East. Most of the book deals with the descendants of righteous Nephi and his brother Laman. The Lamanites warred against the Nephites and destroyed them. So God cursed the Lamanites with a dark skin, and they are the American Indians of today. The last of the Nephite prophets was

Moroni, who hid the golden plates and later appeared as an angel to Joseph Smith at the appointed time to deliver up the records.

The Smithsonian Institution has issued a statement that "Smithsonian archaeologists see no connection between the archaeology of the New World and the subject matter of the Book." Several theories give alternate explanations for the origin of the *Book of Mormon*. Fawn Brodie in *No Man Knows My History* proposes that Joseph created the book himself, using his native genius. Others claim it grew from an unpublished novel about the origin of the American Indians by Solomon Spaulding, who died before the book was printed.[24] They claim that Sidney Rigdon stole the manuscript, assisted Joseph Smith in producing this new American Scripture and then pretended to become a convert after publication of the *Book of Mormon*. However, even late in life, after being excommunicated from the LDS church, Sidney Rigdon still held that he was not its author.[25] A third theory is that Joseph borrowed some of the leading ideas from *View of the Hebrews* by Ethan Smith, published in 1823 and in 1825 in Poultney, Vermont, where Oliver Cowdery (Joseph's scribe for the *Book of Mormon*) lived before coming to New York in 1825. There is obvious proof that Joseph borrowed heavily from the KJV Bible, and he may have borrowed from the Westminster Confession and a book by Josiah Priest called *The Wonders of Nature and Providence Displayed* published in Albany, New York, in 1825. A fourth view is that Joseph actually thought he had these visions and operated under the influence of demonic powers when he received this new gospel. This is a distinct possibility in light of Paul's warning, "But though we, or an angel from heaven, preach any other gospel unto you than that which we have preached unto you, let him be accursed" (Gal 1:8). Perhaps the origin of the *Book of Mormon* contains elements from all of the suggestions listed above.

Doctrine and Covenants. Although Joseph Smith claimed that the *Book of Mormon* was the "keystone" of their religion and that "a man would get nearer to God by abiding by its precepts, than by any other book," numerous distinctive Mormon doctrines are nowhere to be found in it. Harry Ropp in *The Mormon Papers* lists thirteen doctrines not taught in the *Book of Mormon*: "(1) the organizational structure of the church, (2) the Melchizedekian priesthood, (3) the Aaronic priesthood, (4) the plurality of gods, (5) God as an exalted man, (6) a human being's ability to become a god, (7) the three degrees of heaven, (8) the plurality of wives, (9) the Word of Wisdom, (10) the pre-existence of the human spirit, (11) eternal progression, (12) baptism for the dead and (13) celestial marriage."[26] These are introduced through *Doctrine and Covenants (D & C)*, a series of revelations given by Joseph Smith, plus some historical material, a revelation by Brigham Young and a "Manifesto" against polygamy.

The *Doctrine and Covenants* was originally published in 1833 as *A Book of Commandments*. In 1835, it was changed and republished under its present title. Seventy-one sections have been added, but, more important, numerous parts have been changed or removed to support changes Joseph Smith made in his doctrine.

One of the most famous changes is in Section 7 of *D & C*. Joseph acquired a parchment which he "translated" as a message from the pen of John the Apostle. In the original *Book of Commandments* the translation was 111 words shorter. No explanation is given for this. Did the Lord show Joseph that he was a poor translator the first time? Did he suppress evidence the first time? Joseph claimed it was a translation through the Urim and Thummim. Were they defective? This kind of translating work could well damage a prophet's claim to inspiration. While Mormons claim to believe in Joseph Smith's revelations, they have never made it clear which version of those revelations has the Lord's approval.

From 1835 until 1921 "The Lectures on Faith" appeared in all editions of *D & C*. They were carefully prepared and placed there by Joseph Smith himself and were accepted by the quorums of the priesthood as "profitable for doctrine" on August 17, 1835. Then they were dropped without the prophet's written consent or any explanation by the Mormon church. Some of these lessons are embarrassing to the LDS church of today, such as the statement in

"Lecture Third" verse 15 that God "changes not, neither is there variableness with him; but he is the same from everlasting to everlasting, being the same yesterday, today, and forever . . . without variation." This is contrary to their present teaching of eternal progression and God as an exalted man.

The *D & C* also contains prophecies which did not come to pass. Joseph predicted in Section 84 that the New Jerusalem would be built in Zion (Jackson County, Missouri), beginning at the temple lot, "which temple shall be reared in this generation." This prophecy was made in 1832. In December of 1833, he wrote in *D & C* 101:17, 20, "Zion shall not be moved out of her place. . . . And, behold, there is none other place appointed than that which I have appointed." The temple was not reared in Joseph's generation, and the New Jerusalem was not built in Zion.

The Bible gives us a standard against which prophets can be measured. "And if thou say in thine heart, How shall we know the word which the LORD hath not spoken? When a prophet speaketh in the name of the LORD, if the thing follow not, nor come to pass, that is the thing which the LORD hath not spoken, but the prophet hath spoken it presumptuously; thou shalt not be afraid of him" (Deut 18:21-22). Even a prophet who performs miracles or foretells the future accurately is to be rejected if his teachings are contrary to what God has already revealed (see Deut 13:1-5).

Pearl of Great Price. The *Pearl of Great Price* contains "A Selection from the Revelations, Translations, and Narrations of Joseph Smith,"[27] first published in Liverpool, England, in 1851. The most important part of it for our study is the Book of Abraham. In 1835, Michael Chandler opened in Kirtland, Ohio, an exhibit of four Egyptian mummies and some papyri which Joseph and his followers purchased. While Joseph was translating the hieroglyphics (which scholars were still struggling to decipher), Joseph claimed the discovery that some of the papyri were written by Abraham while in Egypt.

For most of Mormon history Blacks were not permitted to hold the priesthood, and they could hope to enter the highest heaven only as servants. The Mormon proof text for this practice was the Book of Abraham 1:26-27. On June 9, 1978, Spencer W. Kimball, President and prophet of the LDS church, issued a revelation that all worthy men could hold the priesthood from this time forth, including Blacks. The Apostle LeGrand Richards explained a major reason for the revelation: "And I might tell you what provoked it in a way. Down in Brazil there is so much Negro blood of the population there that it's hard to get leaders that don't have Negro blood in them, and we just built a temple down there. It's going to be dedicated in October. A lot of those people with Negro blood in them have been raising the money to build that temple. And then if we don't change, then they can't even use it after it's there."[28]

The most important book for determining Joseph Smith's accuracy as a translator is the Book of Abraham. The golden plates and the parchment of John the Apostle are not available for examination, but the papyri for the Book of Abraham, thought to have been lost in the Chicago fire of 1871, were rediscovered and given by the Metropolitan Museum of New York to the Mormon church. At the recommendation of Hugh Nibley, Apostle N. Eldon Tanner turned over photos of these papyri to Dee Jay Nelson, the most qualified Egyptologist among the Mormons. After Nelson's examination, Nibley said, "Latter-day saints owe a debt of gratitude to Mr. Dee Jay Nelson. . . . This is a conscientious and courageous piece of work . . . supplying students with a usable and reliable translation."[29]

What were the results of Nelson's examination? The papyri were no more than Roman period portions of the Egyptian Book of the Dead, giving spells to assist the dead on their journey beyond the grave. In one section, 46 Egyptian characters were translated into 1,125 words. In another place Nelson discovered that one part of a character which means "lake" or "pool" was translated into 76 words with 334 letters. Another character which means "this" in English was translated into 59 words. Joseph's comments on the papyrus's vignettes (which were reproduced as the Book of Abraham "Facsimiles") were no better. Joseph identified an embalming scene for a corpse named Hor (according to the accompanying Egyptian text), as Abraham about to be sacrificed on an Egyptian altar.

Nelson and his family resigned from the LDS church in 1975 after he saw the uselessness of speaking for the truth as an elder within the church. In his letter of resignation he stated, "Following my translation (the first to be published) of the bulk of the hieratic and hieroglyphic Egyptian texts upon the Metropolitan-Joseph Smith Papyri Fragments three of the most eminent Egyptologists now living published corroborating translations. These amply prove the fraudulent nature of the Book of Abraham. . . . We do not wish to be associated with a religious organization which teaches lies."[30]

Nelson also said in an open letter to Mormons about the Book of Abraham, "You have said that when you read it your heart burns within you and that this is your proof of its authenticity. . . . Do you doubt that the ancient Egyptian heart burned any less warmly when he read the Book of the Dead, and how often have I heard Moslems say the same."[31]

Mormon Teachings about God

The most problematic teaching in Mormonism is their doctrine of God. Its main points are absent from or contradicted by both the Bible and the *Book of Mormon*. Notice the following.

Mormons teach that God has a physical body. They believe that God and all other persons first existed as intelligences, which are eternal.[32] The God of this earth was begotten by another god and his wife in the celestial heavens, became a man, lived righteously and was exalted after death to his position as God. Therefore, "God is a glorified and perfected man, a personage of flesh and bones. Inside his tangible body is an eternal spirit."[33]

The only anthropomorphic references to God in the *Book of Mormon* are several references to the finger of God, but as Harry Ropp points out, "This anthropomorphism does not prove that God has a physical body any more than Psalm 91:4 (KJV), 'He shall cover thee with his feathers, and under his wings shalt thou trust,' proves that God is a cosmic chicken."[34] God is called "Great Spirit" (Alma

18:26-28) in the *Book of Mormon*, but he is never referred to as a glorified man.

Mormon proof texts in the Bible for God's having a glorified body of flesh and bones are interesting. Often they quote such phrases as "Moses, whom the LORD knew *face to face*" (Deut 34:10) and "the LORD said . . . I will take away mine *hand*, and thou [Moses] shalt see my *back parts*: but my *face* shall not be seen" (Ex 33:21-23) to prove that God the Father has a physical body. The interesting point is that these Scriptures are about the "LORD" (i.e., Jehovah), which name Mormons say refers to Jesus Christ. How could Christ have a body of flesh and bones before he was born on earth? These and other Bible references to God's body are either anthropomorphisms or descriptions of God temporarily assuming a physical form, but they do not prove that God is a glorified man. By the same argument Mormons should believe that the Holy Ghost has the glorified body of a dove (see Mt 3:16). Of course, they do not.

Mormons teach that God developed from man and that man can become god. God's plan, they say, is for us to become gods like him, where "we would become heavenly parents and have spirit children just as he does."[35] The following poem was first printed in 1919 by the Mormon prophet Lorenzo Snow, but the same doctrine of eternal progression was reportedly stated by Brigham Young at Joseph Smith's funeral:

As man now is, God once was;

As God now is, man may be.

A son of God, like God to be

Would not be robbing deity.[36]

In this scheme the number of gods and worlds is limitless.

Yet Moroni 8:18 in the *Book of Mormon* plainly states, "For I know that God is . . . neither a changeable being; but he is *unchangeable from all eternity to all eternity.*" In Psalm 90:2 we read, "*From everlasting to everlasting,* thou art God." God is always God, and no other God ever existed or ever will. Notice Isaiah 43:10, "*Before* me there was *no God formed, neither* shall there be *after* me." Both the Bible and the *Book of Mormon* refute the idea that God once had a father god, or that we, too, can become gods.

Mormons deny that Jesus was conceived by the Holy Spirit. They teach that we all (including Jesus) are literal descendants of our heavenly Father and one of his wives in heaven. They also teach that Jesus Christ is a literal son of the Father, begotten through the Father's sexual relations with the Virgin Mary. Brigham Young explained that "Jesus Christ was not begotten by the Holy Ghost."[37] He also said, "The birth of the Savior was as natural as the births of our children. . . . [Jesus] was begotten of his Father, as we were of our fathers."[38]

But in keeping with the Bible, Alma 7:10 in the *Book of Mormon* says, "And behold, he [Jesus] shall be born of Mary . . . she being a virgin . . . who shall be overshadowed and *conceive by* the power of the *Holy Ghost*." Matthew 1:18 reads, "When as his mother Mary was espoused to Joseph, before they came together, she was found to be *with child of the Holy Ghost.*"

Mormons deny the unity of the Godhead. They teach that the Father (Elohim), Son (Jehovah or LORD), and Holy Ghost are "three separate individuals, physically distinct from each other" who form "the great presiding council of the universe."[39] They work together, but they are not one God. They are three gods. (How the Holy Ghost became a god without ever assuming a body [necessary for every other male to reach godhood] has never been answered satisfactorily. The Apostle James Talmage argues that God must have a body of parts and passions, because "an immaterial body cannot exist," yet he accepts the idea of the Holy Ghost as being a god who is pure spirit.)[40]

But in Alma 11:29 of the *Book of Mormon*, Amulek responds to Zeezrom's question, "Is there more than one God?" by saying, "No." Amulek explained that he could say nothing contrary to the spirit of God because his information came directly from "an angel of God." Paul in the New Testament said, "There is *none other God but one.* For though there be that are *called gods,* whether in heaven or in earth, (as there be gods many, and lords many,) But to us there is but *one God*" (1 Cor 8:4-6). Mormons claim that there are countless gods, but Paul explains that they are usurpers: so-called gods, but not real. In the "Testimony of Three Witnesses" in the front of the *Book of Mormon* we read, "And the honor be to the Father, and to the Son, and to the Holy Ghost, which is *one God*. Amen." In the *Book of Mormon* in 2 Nephi 31:21 we read, "And now, behold, this is the doctrine of Christ, and *the only and true doctrine* of the Father, and of the Son, and of the Holy Ghost, which is *one God*, without end. Amen." Mormons sometimes object, saying that the *Book of Mormon* means that they are one in purpose, but this is not the way Joseph Smith translated the plates. In all places he leaves out the words "in purpose." The "only and true doctrine" is that the Father, Son and Holy Ghost are actually "one God."

Mormons do not find their doctrines about God in the Bible or the *Book of Mormon*. Their severest doctrinal deviations come from *Doctrine and Covenants* and *Pearl of Great Price*. The "most correct of any book upon the earth," as Joseph Smith called the *Book of Mormon*, contradicts Mormonism. So does the Bible.

A Challenge to Mormons

The strength of the Mormon church is in the commitment of its adherents, in the positive image projected by its dedicated young missionaries and in the healthy family life displayed by the Mormon community. The weaknesses are harder to detect, but they certainly exist.

People who take the Bible as their sole authority in matters of faith and practice can readily conclude that Mormonism is inconsistent with genuine Christianity. But Mormon believers are not limited to the Bible. Therefore Mormons need to face some of the difficulties that arise within the context of their own authority structure. Here is a summary of a few we have examined:

1. The Mormon scriptures have undergone extensive emenda-

tion, even though Mormon teaching about these scriptures does not allow for such changes.

2. Some teaching in later scriptures, such as *Doctrine and Covenants,* disagrees with teaching in earlier scriptures, such as the *Book of Mormon.*

3. Some Mormon prophecies, particularly by Joseph Smith, have not come true.

4. The textual basis for the Book of Abraham in the *Pearl of Great Price* does not stand up under scholarly examination.

5. Joseph Smith himself told conflicting stories of his First Vision.

6. Modern archaeology is not compatible with the *Book of Mormon*'s story of the Lamanites and Nephites.

7. The subjective feeling that the *Book of Mormon* is the Word of God is not an adequate reason for belief.

To Mormons who read this chapter I would like to offer encouragement. I know you are serious about finding the truth or you would not have read this far. May I challenge you to go further?

Look again at the basis of your faith. Examine the scriptures on which it is built. Check to see if what I have said about Mormonism is true. Read a full book-length analysis of the Mormon faith (see the reading list at the end of this book).

Then examine the alternative—faith in the God of the Bible. Read the New Testament, especially the Gospels. Get a clear view of the Jesus of the Bible. Pray that God will lead you to the truth wherever it is to be found. An excellent presentation of the Christian faith is found in John Stott's *Basic Christianity* which is available in most Christian bookstores.

Jesus said, "If ye continue in my word, then are ye my disciples indeed; and ye shall know the truth, and the truth shall make you free" (Jn 8:31-32). It is Jesus' word we must know and heed. May we all be equal to the challenge.

9

Transcendental Meditation

David Haddon

*It is wise to know not only what one
is going to do, but where,
as a result, one is going to end up.*
Maharishi Mahesh Yogi

MAHARISHI MAHESH YOGI, the originator of Transcendental Meditation (TM), often makes commonsensical observations on life with the down-to-earth appeal of proverbial wisdom.[1] It is not his engaging personality, however, but the mental and spiritual effects of TM that lead us to consider both what one does and where one is going to end up as a result of its practice.

First, where does TM come from? After Maharishi's graduation from the University of Allahabad, India, in 1941 with a B.S. in physics, he became the favorite disciple of one of the chief religious leaders of India, Swami Brahmananda Saraswati ("Guru Dev"), who was the Shankaracharya of Jyotir Math (a Hindu monastery). Here Maharishi mastered yoga and absorbed the monistic world view of the great ninth-century Hindu reformer, Shankara, who taught the absolute unity of all being (that is, that "All is

One"). Maharishi's Science of Creative Intelligence (SCI), the theoretical aspect of TM, is a restatement in semiscientific language of the principles of Shankara's monism.[2] Thus, Hindu monism or pantheism is the underlying philosophy of the entire movement.

TM in America

When Guru Dev died in 1953, Maharishi withdrew to a cave in the Himalayas. After two years of isolation there, Maharishi emerged and began teaching in south India. Early in 1959, he set out for the United States with the simple technique of yogic meditation for popular use now called TM. By midsummer a branch of his Spiritual Regeneration Movement (SRM) was begun in Los Angeles.[3] Since then a million and a half Americans are said to have learned TM and about 14,000 of these to have become teachers for Maharishi's World Plan Executive Council (WPEC), the legal name of the movement in the United States. Worldwide, about two million have been trained in the technique.

In its heyday in the midseventies, TM was called the McDonald's of meditation because of its extravagantly successful packaging of Eastern meditation for the American mass market. The key to TM's success was its presentation as a scientifically verified, effortless technique of self-improvement totally unrelated to religion. Maharishi had shrewdly discerned that in America science was regarded as the highest authority. He therefore shifted the presentation of TM from the religious orientation of his original SRM to the scientific approach of his Students' International Meditation Society (SIMS).

Since 1976, however, TM has suffered a decline in popularity which may be traced, in part, to its inability to deliver on exaggerated claims of the universal benefits and even supernatural powers conferred by TM. The TM-Sidhi program launched in 1977 purports to teach meditators to levitate or "fly" and to vanish at will. Such claims have tarnished the scientific image of TM which it, nevertheless, doggedly strives to maintain in the face of this obviously occult activity as well as its Hindu background. An even more telling blow to TM's image was the 1977 federal court ruling that TM/SCI courses were a religious teaching under the Establishment Clause of the U.S. Constitution. That decision implied the use of deception in the presentation of TM. It also cut off government funds for teaching TM in public schools.

Despite such reverses to the movement, Maharishi International University (MIU) was able to raise $8 million to add a Washington, D.C., branch to its Fairfield, Iowa, campus in 1980. As a result, the old Annapolis Hotel in Washington now houses the fledgling MIU College of Natural Law.

Much of the financial support for the TM movement comes from course fees, which are substantial. The basic TM course, for example, costs $250 for an adult and $175 for a college student, while the eight-week TM-Sidhi course costs a cool $3,000.

Researchers Investigate TM

Beginning in 1970, preliminary scientific research suggested that TM lowered metabolism and induced relaxation during its practice. Some reduction in blood pressure was observed in hypertensives who practiced TM. Other studies indicated that TM helped some people reduce drug abuse. MIU has used these and many other studies uncritically in order to build an image of TM as a scientific panacea whose practice effortlessly provides an amazing array of benefits ranging from increased intelligence to a reversal of the aging process.

Some researchers have criticized MIU's handling of research data as giving only the most favorable possible view of TM. Studies of TM with results and interpretations contradicting studies presented by MIU have been published by scientists independent of MIU.

Researchers have shown, for example, that the relaxation and stress reduction associated with TM can be produced just as well by other forms of resting such as sitting quietly with eyes closed. One such study by Jonathan C. Smith of Michigan State University led him to conclude that the "crucial therapeutic component of

TM is not the TM exercise."[4] He believed that the subject's expectation of relief, the placebo effect, was the cause of similar reductions of anxiety in both meditating and resting groups.

Some attempts to reproduce the favorable results of TM published by MIU have been unsuccessful. For example, one of the claims made for TM is that it increases intelligence and improves grades. At the University of Illinois at Chicago Circle, however, researchers compared the grades of groups of meditators with matched control groups for one and two quarters. They concluded that "no effect upon grades was demonstrated for TM training."[5]

From the above examples, it is apparent that the claims of benefits from TM, though based on scientific studies, cannot be uncritically accepted at face value. Where the benefits are genuine, they may be due to simple rest, to the placebo effect or to other factors. And if the benefits claimed cannot be duplicated by studies independent of the TM movement, they cannot be considered scientifically established.

On the other hand, negative effects of TM have come to the surface since Leon Otis of Stanford Research Institute noticed that some meditators suffered from increased anxiety, confusion and depression.[6] And researcher Arnold Lazarus of Rutgers University reported that he had encountered a woman who had attempted suicide after a weekend training course in TM.[7] These and other scientists say that TM is actually harmful to some people in contradiction to Maharishi's claim that TM is universally beneficial.

The Practice of TM
In order to begin TM, one first attends two introductory lectures that present TM as a nonreligious mental technique for gaining deep rest and a variety of "scientifically verified" benefits. After the lectures, candidates for initiation into TM pay their fee and are told to bring flowers, fruit and a white handkerchief to the initiation ceremony.

At the ceremony, in a small, candlelit room filled with incense, the flowers, fruit and handkerchief are offered to Guru Dev on the altar before his image. The teacher sings a Sanskrit hymn of praise to the Hindu deities personified in Guru Dev. In English translation, the portion of the hymn that accompanies the offering of the flowers, for example, begins:

GURU in the glory of BRAHMA, GURU in the glory of VISHNU, GURU in the glory of the great LORD SHIVA, GURU in the glory of the personified transcendental fulness of BRAHMAN, to Him, to SHRI GURU DEV adorned with glory, I bow down.[8]

It is clear even from this brief excerpt from the text that Guru Dev is being worshiped as a divinity through his image over the altar. But the second commandment says, "You shall not make for yourself an idol. . . . You shall not bow down to them or worship them" (Ex 20:4-5 NIV). In view of this commandment, many professing Christians and Jews would have avoided becoming involved in TM had the idolatrous character of this ceremony ever been frankly acknowledged by its sponsors. The purpose of secrecy and deception about the religious nature of TM, of course, is to encourage just such unwitting involvement.

After the hymn, the initiator kneels and invites the candidate to kneel to receive the secret word or mantra which is recited during meditation. Most, if not all, of the mantras are the names of Hindu deities. Advanced techniques add Sanskrit words such as *Shri* ("Lord") and *namah* ("I bow down") to render the mantras into phrases of worship of the gods invoked.[9] The claim that TM is nonreligious is a lie of massive proportions that touches the conscience of every teacher of TM. Mercy requires Christians lovingly to confront such persons with their sin and Christ's offer of forgiveness (2 Tim 2:24-26).

Not until the last of three sessions of instruction following the initiation ceremony, however, does the beginning meditator learn something of the spiritual goals of TM. Only after the candidate has paid his fee and learned to silently recite his mantra to produce the altered consciousness of meditation are the possibilities of attaining the permanently altered states of Cosmic-consciousness discussed.

In his commentary on the Bhagavad-Gita, Maharishi explains the basic reason that TM is presented as one thing to nonmeditators and as another to those who have begun meditation:

If the *enlightened* man wants to bless one who is *ignorant*, he should . . . try to lift him up from there by giving him the key to transcending [i.e., TM], so that he may gain bliss-consciousness and experience the Reality of Life. *He should not tell him about the level of the realized because it would only confuse him.*[10]

TM, then, is an esoteric practice since it sets its teachers on a level of understanding above others who are called "ignorant." Maharishi goes even further to say that "one who has not realized the truth of activity or the truth of silence [both via TM] does not deserve to be called a man."[11] Maharishi thus distinguishes meditators and nonmeditators as the human from the nonhuman. The potential for religious persecution latent in such a distinction is obvious and appalling.

Conditioned Enlightenment

A primary goal of TM is to alter permanently the meditator's perception of the world until it harmonizes with Maharishi's pantheistic world view. Maharishi himself admits that TM is a conditioning process for this purpose. Concerning the "enlightened" state of Cosmic-consciousness, he writes:

This [state] is brought about by regularly interrupting the constant activity of the waking state of consciousness with periods of silence in transcendental consciousness [via TM]. When, *through this practice, the nervous system has been permanently conditioned to maintain these two states together,* then consciousness remains always centered in the Self.[12]

As the meditator becomes conditioned to perceive reality as conforming to the monist principle that "All is One," he is attaining to the state of God-consciousness. Reason is abandoned in favor of mystical paradox, not only as a matter of abstract principle, but because of the subjective effect on perception of the conditioning process of TM. At this point the interference of meditation with logical thought is total in the sense that reason is rejected in favor of mystical experience as a means for discerning the ultimate truth about reality.

The mystical "enlightenment" of the altered states of consciousness, then, is a matter of permanently conditioning the nervous system to a nonrational perception of the world. Meditators are often told that in TM they gain direct experience of "Reality," but this claim that the human nervous system can provide direct experience of ultimate reality depends on the unproven premise that man has access to ultimate reality within himself. However convincing the mystical experience may be subjectively, it can never prove this premise about man. The Jewish philosopher and sometime mystic Martin Buber in *Between Man and Man* provides a cogent alternative interpretation for this kind of mystical experience:

> Now from my own unforgettable experience I know well that there is a state in which . . . we experience an undivided unity. But I do not know—what the soul willingly imagines . . . —that in this I had attained to a union with the primal being. . . . In the honest and sober account of the responsible understanding the unity is nothing but the unity of this soul of mine, whose "ground" I have reached . . . and not . . . "Being."[13]

TM as Religion

Supposedly one needs no faith to begin TM. But in Maharishi's inner teaching the initiate learns that "the practice of transcendental meditation . . . brings faith to the faithless."[14] Moreover, to attain to "enlightenment" the meditator must gain faith in his teacher and in what Maharishi calls "God" as well as in his own experience of meditation. Maharishi explains:

> There are three fields of faith: faith in oneself, faith in the teacher and faith in God. *Faith in oneself* is necessary so that one does not begin to doubt *one's own experience. Faith in the teacher* enables one to accept the fundamentals of the teaching. . . . *Faith in God* [the impersonal absolute] protects man's heart and mind and ensures that steady progress which is so important in the life

of a seeker. . . . For ultimate fulfillment in God-consciousness *the greatest faith is needed.*[15]

Contrary to the way TM is presented to the public, it is apparent that TM is intended gradually to build faith first in "one's own experience" of TM and then in the "teacher." Finally these two interact to produce personal commitment to TM as a way of life and faith in Shankara's monistic concept of "God" as an all-encompassing unity of being.

On the basis of its nonreligious claims, courses in the Science of Creative Intelligence and TM (SCI/TM) were begun in public schools from New York to California in 1971. In February of 1976, however, a group of Christians in New Jersey filed suit in federal court against the teaching of SCI/TM courses in their local public schools because of their recognition of its Hindu religious character. Defendants included Maharishi Mahesh Yogi, his WPEC, the Secretary of the U.S. Department of Health, Education and Welfare (in view of federal financing), and state and local school officials.

The case was finally decided in December 1977, when the U.S. District Court Judge, H. Curtis Meanor, pronounced the judgment that "the Science of Creative Intelligence/Transcendental Meditation . . . and the puja [initiation] ceremony, are all religious in nature within the context of the Establishment Clause of the First Amendment of the United States Constitution, and teaching thereof in the New Jersey public schools is therefore unconstitutional." The defendants were permanently enjoined from the teaching of SCI/TM, the use of the SCI textbook and practice of TM in New Jersey public schools.[16] Since Judge Meanor's ruling was upheld in the appeals court, it stands as a strong precedent against the use of public funds for the teaching of TM or similar practices throughout the United States.

Despite this definitive court ruling on the religious nature of TM, Maharishi as well as his followers still maintains the imposture that TM has nothing to do with religion. His decision to follow this course seems to be accepted, because he is viewed as a messiah whose World Plan will save the world.

In 1972, Maharishi revealed his World Plan whose seven goals include, among others:

5. To solve the problems of crime, drug abuse, and all behavior that brings unhappiness to the family of man.

6. To bring fulfillment to the economic aspirations of individuals and society.

7. To achieve the spiritual goals of mankind in this generation.

From the Bible, Christians know that a day will come when such millennial conditions will prevail on earth—when Jesus Christ returns. Until that day, such messianic claims to establish an "Age of Enlightenment," as Maharishi puts it, are both hopeless and blasphemous. Hopeless because it is doomed to founder on the rocks of human sinfulness, and blasphemous because they disregard God's revelation of his will to restore fallen humanity to its rightful place through his King alone, Jesus Christ (Psalm 2).

Maharishi's Theology

Those who are concerned to know where a person may end up when he begins TM should consider what Maharishi says about "God." He writes that "God is found in two phases of reality: as a supreme Being of absolute, eternal nature and as a personal God at the highest level of phenomenal creation."[17] Yet as a consistent monist, Maharishi goes on to identify the "supreme Being" and the creation. He writes that the "impersonal God . . . is the essential constituent of creation."[18] By making God a part of the creation, Maharishi equates Creator and creature and thus fulfills the essence of the biblical definition of idolatry (Rom 1:25). This leads naturally to the further idolatry of self-worship. This tendency is apparent in Maharishi's claim that "each individual is, in his true nature, the impersonal God."[19]

The personal God revealed in the Bible never acknowledges man as God or a part of God. Yahweh's exclusive personal claim to Deity is proclaimed by the prophet Isaiah: "For thus says the

143

LORD, who created the heavens (he is God!), . . . 'I am the LORD, and there is no other' " (Is 45:18).

A person's view of Jesus Christ is another crucial index of his theology. In his *Meditations* Maharishi writes, "I don't think Christ ever suffered or Christ could suffer. . . . It's a pity that Christ is talked of in terms of suffering."[20] Christ's rebuke to some of his own followers who failed to recognize the prophetic necessity of his suffering was, "O foolish men, and slow of heart to believe all that the prophets have spoken! Was it not necessary that the Christ should suffer these things and enter into his glory?" (Lk 24:25-26). To deny the sufferings of Christ is to reject Christ and to receive his rebuke. Rightly understanding the suffering and death of Christ is of first importance for theology and life because, according to the Bible, faith in Christ's sacrifice is the basis for knowing God (1 Cor 15:3; Heb 9—10).

Finally, because Maharishi's "supreme Being" is not a person, it lacks the abilities of the humblest person on earth who can speak, act and love. Maharishi admits the impotence of this "God" when he writes, "The Absolute is said to be almighty [but] . . . being everything, It cannot do anything or know anything."[21] The Absolute "cannot do anything," yet Maharishi inexplicably assigns it causal status for the world: "It is through the power of the impersonal God that the world was, is and will be."[22]

Obviously the pantheist is faced with the same problem as the materialist when confronted by the need for a causal explanation for the order of the universe and for human personality. The (personal) effect that is man requires as its cause not merely something greater in extent and energy, but something greater also in the powers of knowing and doing unique to persons. Only when the one God, the Creator, is acknowledged as the Person who is supreme over all reality does an explanation for the world and for man become possible.

Where Does TM End Up?
Maharishi has specifically warned his followers of one particular

hazard of meditation that should be mentioned here as a possible effect of TM. In *Science of Being and Art of Living,* he advises against invoking spirits or acting as a medium because "to receive this . . . power . . . one must give oneself completely to that spirit's influence."[23] One reason that such a warning is necessary is that the meditative state resembles the state sought by mediums in order to contact spirits. On a Christian view, the spirits involved are demons and the hazard recognized that of demon possession. Some former meditators do, indeed, testify to frightening encounters with spirits. So we should seriously consider the possibility that the suspension of conscious direction of the faculties in meditation opens one to Satanic spiritual influences.

People who do TM end up in a variety of places; many drop out of TM entirely. TM in itself, however, is intended to lead to specific goals which only those who develop a commitment to TM as a way of life are deeply aware of. These goals include, as we have seen, the states of permanently altered consciousness or "enlightenment." For the elite who attain to the states beyond Cosmic-consciousness, however, the supposed goal may become a final "liberation" from personal existence (at death) in the impersonal Absolute. Maharishi affirms that for "a realized man . . . death is just a silent declaration of no return—no return to the cycle of birth and death."[24] This ancient Hindu doctrine of escape from the cycle of reincarnation into the "bliss-consciousness" of the "impersonal God" describes the ultimate, though often ignored, goal of TM.

But does the denial of the personhood of God (the "supreme Being") that leads to this goal come from a true vision of reality held by Maharishi or from a deceptive process of conditioning of which Maharishi is perhaps a chief victim? Having begun a spiritual pursuit on the impersonal path of mantramic meditation, the meditator naturally comes to an impersonal conclusion about the nature of God. The conclusion that God is not a person is built into the impersonal technique of reciting a word without regard for its meaning, because if two persons are to become acquainted, they must communicate their thoughts in meaningful words. If God, the Supreme Being, is a Person as the Bible teaches, we can only come to know him through personal communication such as in prayer or Bible reading.

By reading the Gospels, for example, one learns that Jesus Christ is called the divine Word and that he taught *his disciples* to talk to God as Father in simple but rationally connected words like those of the Lord's Prayer (Mt 6:7-13). Jesus specifically rejected repetitive verbal exercises like mantramic meditation as means to God when he said, "When you are praying, do not use meaningless repetition, as the Gentiles do" (Mt 6:7 NASB). For those not yet his disciples, Christ presented himself as the personal way to the personal Father (Mt 11:27; Jn 14:6).

Deep Rest and Personal Fulfillment in Christ
The question of whether the Supreme Being is a personal God or impersonal being is of the greatest practical importance in the quest for personal fulfillment. By denying the personhood of God, the Supreme Being, Maharishi minimizes the importance of personality and denies the ultimate survival and significance of persons. In contrast, the Christian acknowledgment of God as the Person in whose image man was created maximizes the importance of persons. The biblical promises of resurrection of the body, of judgment and of eternal reward in heaven or eternal banishment in hell all imply the significance and eternal duration of human personality. Christ's bodily resurrection from the dead is evidence of his Deity and of the Father's acceptance of his sacrificial death for the sins of mankind. And thus his resurrection provides an objective ground for confidence in the ultimate triumph over sin and death promised to his followers.

Faith in Christ also offers deep rest to the mind and body burdened by fear, alienation and guilt. According to the Bible, alienation from and moral guilt before the personal God whose holiness is absolute are man's basic problems. The anxiety and stress that TM relieves are mere symptoms of the insidious underlying disorder the Bible calls sin. Sin at its root is man's willful refusal to acknowledge and serve the personal God and Creator as supreme. The pantheist's denial of personality to the Supreme Being is thus an expression of sin. But people can be liberated from this tendency to disregard the Person of God, because one day about A.D. 30 Jesus Christ suffered death for our sin on a cross outside Jerusalem.

Because he was raised from the dead the third day, Jesus still calls, "Come to me, all who labor and are heavy laden, and I will give you rest" (Mt 11:28). The rest that Christ offers reaches to the very root of our being by healing our alienation from God. That is why the apostle Paul can write to believers: "Once you were alienated from God and were enemies in your minds because of your evil behavior. But now he has reconciled you by Christ's physical body through death to present you holy in his sight" (Col 1:21-22 NIV).

Just as the impersonal can never explain the existence of a person, neither can a person find his complete fulfillment in the impersonal experience of Eastern meditation. Personal fulfillment in life is achieved in a personal relationship of love with the personal Fatheough his only Son, Jesus Christ. Such a relationship is begun by the personal act of speaking to the Lord Jesus in faith while turning away from the self to God in heaven. By thus acting on the basis of the objective, historical record of what God has done in Christ for the redemption of man, one also makes the subjective discovery that "reality . . . is found in Christ" (Col 2:17 NIV). Reason and experience are integrated by this relationship with the Creator who made both mind and body.

A full comprehension of the Person of Jesus Christ, then, depends on both an intellectual understanding of the revelation of Scripture about him and a personal experience of spiritual rebirth through him. Then we can grasp the biblical revelation of Jesus Christ as God Incarnate—the Creator and Sustainer of the universe made flesh. A majestic passage of Scripture that so reveals Christ says of him:

He is the image of the invisible God, the firstborn over all creation. For by him all things were created. . . . He is before all
things, and in him all things hold together. . . . He is the beginning and the firstborn from among the dead, so that in everything he might have the supremacy. For God was pleased to have
all his fullness dwell in him, and through him to reconcile to
himself all things, . . . by making peace through his blood, shed
on the cross. (Col 1:15-20 NIV)

Against those who deny that the divine fullness is to be found only
in Christ, the Bible warns: "See to it that no one takes you captive
through hollow and deceptive philosophy, which depends on human tradition and the basic principles of this world rather than on
Christ" (Col 2:8 NIV). Only the concrete, personal fullness of Deity
that is Christ can be the wellspring of fulfillment for mankind: "For
in Christ all the fullness of the Deity lives in bodily form, and you
have this fullness in Christ" (Col 2:9-10 NIV).

Maharishi was certainly right in saying, "It is wise to know . . .
where . . . one is going to end up." It is ironic, therefore, that he has
so persistently concealed from the public both the religious basis
and the ultimate spiritual goal of TM—the annihilation of personal
existence in the impersonal Absolute. Many meditators are un-
aware that they have embarked on a dynamic spiritual path whose
final goal is loss of personhood in the Absolute.

The biblical view of where one is going to end up as a result
of the practice of TM is even darker than that of extinction in
the impersonal Absolute of being. If, as often seems to happen,
TM leads one to accept Maharishi's World Plan as a substitute for
the gospel, to accept Maharishi as a substitute for Jesus as Messiah, or to accept oneself as "God" or part of "God," the judgment of God is clear. Those who refuse to know the personal God of
Abraham as supreme and who therefore "do not obey the gospel
of our Lord Jesus . . . shall suffer the punishment of eternal destruction and exclusion from the presence of the Lord (2 Thess
1:8-9). As a substitute system of spirituality, however, TM has
special power to blind its practicers to the truth of the gospel and

thus to encourage their fatal disobedience to it.

Jesus presented a very different goal in a very different way. He frankly challenged prospective followers to give him their very lives from the outset. He promised them that even in the midst of persecution there would be forgiveness, peace and joyful fulfillment through an unending personal relationship with himself and God the Father. This relationship is a present experience to be brought to final perfection at Christ's return in glory and power. Through the word of the gospel and the Spirit of Christ, his promise of continuing personal communion still reaches to every person who will receive Jesus Christ as Lord and Savior.

10
Unification Church (Moonies)
J. Isamu Yamamoto

*No heroes in the past, no saints or
holy men in the past, like Jesus, or Confucius,
have excelled us.*
Sun Myung Moon

IN MANY BUSY AIRPORTS, ON STREET corners, college campuses
and shopping centers, Americans are confronted by the smiling
faces of young converts to the Unification Church, headed by Sun
Myung Moon. Neatly dressed, kind and warm, they put their best
foot forward.

What lies behind their very pleasant image? Who is Sun Myung
Moon? What does he teach? Is the Unification Church just another
Christian denomination, or does it depart from biblical teaching?
What is life like for a follower of Moon? And how should Christians
respond to this movement?

Sun Myung Moon
Sun Myung Moon was born January 6, 1920, the second son of
eight children.[1] His father was a farmer and a Presbyterian. When

Moon finished primary school in his home village of Kwangju Sangsa Ri (in what is now North Korea), his parents sent him to high school in Seoul where he began to attend a Pentecostal church.

Moon says that on Easter 1936, while deep in prayer on a Korean mountainside, he saw Jesus, who told him he had been chosen to finish the work Jesus had begun. For the next nine years he prepared himself for that mission. Among some Pentecostal Christians in the underground church in Pyongyang, there had recently been prophecy of a Korean messiah. So the local populace was fertile ground for this idea.

During World War 2, Moon attended Waseda University in Tokyo, where he studied electrical engineering. It is unclear whether he actually graduated.

In 1944 Moon went back to North Korea and succeeded in gathering some followers. Later, in 1946, he traveled to South Korea where he met Paik Moon Kim, whose name means "100 Gold Letters." This man, six years Moon's senior, fancied himself the fulfillment of the Korean messianic expectations and publicly declared himself a savior. In Paju, a town north of Seoul and near the 38th parallel, Kim founded the Israel Soodo Won (Israel Monastery). Moon studied in this community for six months, formulating his own teachings, which were subsequently set forth in the *Divine Principle.* He then returned to his followers in Pyongyang, and in 1946, after he had established the "Broad Sea Church," he began preaching.

During this period Moon changed his birth name Yong Myung Moon to Sun Myung Moon. Yong can be translated "dragon," Myung means "shining," and Moon is a common surname meaning "letter," "character" or "writing." The character for Sun signifies "propriety" or "goodness." Since 1946, then, Moon has gone by a name which means "Shining Proper Letter."

During 1946-50 Moon was in prison for a time in North Korea. Moon himself claims that because of his anticommunist activities he was imprisoned twice when the communists swept into North

Korea. He further states that he was tortured for three years in a communist prison. In the booklet *The Heart of Our Father* Moon's suffering for his faith is likened to the suffering of Christ. After he had attracted a small group of disciples in war-torn North Korea, "the police came and an innocent man [Moon] received a terrible beating, pints of blood flowed from an internal injury. He lost consciousness. His broken body was thrown outside the Daedong Police Station onto the frozen ground. Other disciples carried it away for a Christian burial. Remarkably it still breathed. In three days he began to preach again. The catacomb existence of the underground saint began."[2] Others say that he was imprisoned for adultery and bigamy, asserting that Moon's anticommunist work was not organized until 1962.

Just as the facts are uncertain as to the cause and the circumstances of his imprisonment, so are there various reports concerning Moon's deliverance out of the hands of the communists. One account states that in June 1950 Moon escaped when a bombardment by the United Nations Forces caused his communist jailers to flee. Another is that in the winter of 1950-51 he was released from prison by the United Nations Forces at Hung Nam.

Whatever the facts of his release, it is known that Moon returned to South Korea with several followers. He settled at Pusan where he became a harbor laborer between 1950 and 1954. During this time, he began to teach the Principles formulated by himself and a former medical student in Pusan named Hye Won Yoo, who was paralyzed so badly that he could not even sit. Yoo both wrote the principles of this new religion and invented the air gun which brought prosperity to Moon. Yoo died about 1970.

In 1954 Moon established his church in Seoul. In Korean it is called the Tong-il-Kyo and in English "The Holy Spirit Association for the Unification of World Christianity" (or simply the Unification Church). In 1957 he published a book entitled *Divine Principle*, the new revelation he claimed to have received from God. It was revised in 1966 and published in English in the United States that same year and again in 1973.

In 1954 Moon's wife of ten years left him because, he claims, "she could not comprehend my mission."[3] Later, on July 4, 1955, in Seoul, the police imprisoned Moon and his chief members for three months. His indictment was initially draft dodging but later changed to adultery and promiscuity. At that time most of his followers were men who had left their wives and had joined a new Unification community. Students and faculty accused of participation in "the scandalous rites of the Unification Church" were asked to leave the universities. Moon was acquitted and now claims to have been persecuted for his anticommunist beliefs.

In March 1960 Moon married again. The union between Sun Myung Moon and Hak Ja Han is called "the Marriage of the Lamb." Moon is called the "Father of the universe" and his wife is called the "Mother of the universe." Moon declared that twenty-one is a special number which symbolizes perfection and that within twenty-one years after 1960 his current wife would bear him twelve children, one for each disciple and gate in heaven. In February 1981, their twelfth child was born. Thus his family goals have been fulfilled. Each child is considered sinless, and they along with their parents are said to herald the coming perfection of humanity.

Moon arrived in Los Angeles in December 1971 to commence his seven-city "Day of Hope" tour across the United States. His first speaking engagement was in New York in January 1972. He called Americans to abandon their denominational religions for a real relationship with God through the Second Coming of Christ and to give up their fragmented nationalism for the building of the Kingdom of Heaven on earth. Thus he started his mission in America, a task which he states God has called him to.

1981 was again proclaimed a significant year. That would be the year the New Kingdom of Heaven on Earth would begin and the world would acknowledge Moon as the Lord of the Second Advent. The New Kingdom did not come, however, in 1981. Instead, Moon quietly told his followers that it would come in 2001. "The reason for the delay, Moon said, was that the world was not yet ready for the new age, because of a failure of faith by outsiders and by his own church's failure to convert them."[4]

Moon had hoped to establish the Kingdom of God on earth by realizing three goals. Each would have helped establish the Kingdom of God on earth by 1981, but each hope was only partially fulfilled. He had hoped to enlarge his church so that he could easily conduct a mass marriage of 10,000 couples. He had hoped to continue the fantastic financial growth of his church in America. And he had hoped to develop ties with evangelical Christians so that his church could be accepted by the traditional Christian community.

On July 1, 1982, Moon united 2,075 couples in marriage in New York's Madison Square Garden, a happy occasion for Moon and his church. Nevertheless, although close to 8,000 more couples were to be married in the following months, there was still disappointment for Moon in that his timetable was not met. From three missionaries who came to the United States in 1959, the Unification Church claims about 10,000 active members, far fewer than the number Moon had hoped for in 1971.

Since 1973, Moon has been a permanent resident of the United States. During that time he and his church have amassed a financial empire including an estate and a seminary in New York, the Diplomat National Bank, the New Yorker Hotel and the *Washington Times,* as well as other real estate and industries. Nevertheless, although his church has survived attacks by the media, deprogrammers and parent groups, Moon has had major difficulties with governmental agencies. A setback occurred on July 16, 1982, when he was sentenced to eighteen months in jail and a $25,000 fine for tax evasion.

Finally, Moon has sponsored numerous dialogs between Unification theologians and Christians, particularly evangelicals. Some of these conferences have been at such alluring places as the Bahamas, the Canary Islands, Hawaii, Lisbon and Athens. Although many evangelicals have attended and have appreciated the friendliness of their hosts, they have maintained that there can be no compatibility between Unification theology and biblical Christianity, particularly regarding Christology. In effect, Moon's attempt to move his church into the mainstream of Christian denominations has failed.

The Moon Doctrine

The primary document containing the basic tenets and doctrines of the Unification Church is the *Divine Principle*. Members of the church believe that this book contains revelations from God to Moon: "With the fullness of time, God has sent His messenger to resolve the fundamental questions of life and the universe. His name is Sun Myung Moon" (DP 16).[5] The *Divine Principle* serves a twofold purpose: It indoctrinates adherents of the Unification Church into a particular line of belief, and it undermines all forms of present New Testament theology, particularly that of orthodox Christianity. The *Divine Principle* recognizes that Christians may be unhappy to learn that a new revelation is necessary. Yet, since the Bible is "not the truth itself, but a textbook teaching the truth," it must not be regarded as "absolute in every detail" (DP 9).

The specific teaching of the *Divine Principle* can best be divided into three areas: the first Adam, the second Adam and the Lord of the Second Advent. The first Adam and Eve were God's initial human creations who fell into sin. The second Adam was Jesus Christ who died on the cross because of the faithlessness of the Jews. The Lord of the Second Advent is the Messiah who must come to establish the Kingdom of Heaven here on earth. These three Adams comprise God's plan for fulfilling the original goals of creation.

The First Adam. In order to understand the message of the *Divine Principle*, we must grasp the fundamental theme underlying all of its basic concepts: Whether positive or negative (DP 21), external or internal (DP 21), Yin or Yang (DP 26), all concepts are broken down into dualities of which male and female is the thread that sews them all together. Creation itself is understood after this pattern, for God, prior to creating the universe, existed as "the internal masculine subject." In making the universe, he created an "external feminine object" (DP 25). God as subject gives love to the object, which returns beauty to the subject. This brings perfect joy to the subject, and the relationship between God and creation is fulfilled.

God's highest expression of this duality within creation itself was to be the relationship between man and woman. The first man was Adam; the first woman was Eve. God created them spiritually immature as brother and sister. He intended for them to assume a subject/object relationship with himself in their growth to spiritual perfection. Thereafter, as husband and wife, Adam and Eve were supposed to establish the Kingdom of Heaven on earth through their offspring. The goal of creation was thwarted, however, by Adam and Eve's sin. According to the *Divine Principle,* for centuries no one has understood the true story of the fall of Adam and Eve. We have believed that the transgression took place when they ate the fruit of the tree of knowledge of good and evil. The *Divine Principle,* however, claims that the tree of life symbolizes perfected Adam and the tree of knowledge symbolizes Eve.

The *Divine Principle* explains the fall this way. When man was created, Lucifer became extremely envious of God's love for man. He also saw Eve's great beauty and lusted after her. At this time Lucifer had not fallen himself, but because of jealousy and lust he entered into an unlawful relationship with Eve. Their sexual intercourse constitutes the *spiritual* fall of man as well as the fall of Lucifer.

When Eve participated in an illicit relationship with Lucifer, she received spiritual insight and realized that she had violated the purpose of creation. She knew then that her intended spouse was not Lucifer but Adam. Subsequently she had intercourse with Adam in an attempt to restore her position with God. Adam, however, was still spiritually immature. Consequently they entered into a relationship which constituted the *physical* fall of man. So there is a dual aspect to the fall: a *spiritual* fall and a *physical* fall. Both of them have to do with sexuality.

The *Divine Principle* argues for the sexual nature of the fall as

157

follows. Prior to the fall, Adam and Eve were naked and were not ashamed; after the fall they were ashamed of their nakedness and so they sewed fig leaves into aprons to cover their lower parts. This tells us that their sexuality was involved in the fall because, the *Divine Principle* argues, "it is the nature of man to conceal an area of transgression. They covered their sexual parts, clearly indicating that they were ashamed of the sexual areas of their bodies because they had committed sin through them" (DP 72).

As a result of Eve's illicit love affair with Satan, Cain was born, symbolizing man's relationship with Satan. The political configuration of this relationship has culminated in communism. Abel, as the fruit of her second love affair with Adam, symbolizes man's relationship with God. The political configuration of this relationship has culminated in democracy. Thus, communism is the expression of Satan and democracy the expression of God.

The fall of man constituted a problem for God, for by it God's plans were thwarted. Since the fall, it has been God's will to restore people to himself through a *spiritual* and *physical* redemption. People in every age, from Noah to Abraham to David, have failed to obey God. Finally there lived an obedient man. His name was Jesus.

The Second Adam. The *Divine Principle* states that about 400 years in advance of Jesus, God sent Malachi to the Jewish nation to prepare them for the coming of the Messiah (DP 423). Meanwhile, God had Gautama, called the Buddha, and Confucius prepare the Asian world and Socrates the Hellenist world for the coming of the Messiah. All religions and cultures were to unify under the acceptance of Jesus. God's will, however, was tragically thwarted by the crucifixion of Jesus.

The reason for his crucifixion is now revealed. The major cause which kept the Jews from believing in Jesus was John the Baptist's ignorance of the providence of God. Instead of serving and ministering to Jesus, John encouraged disbelief in Jesus among the Jews.

It should be noted that the *Divine Principle* does not claim that Jesus sinned or failed to obey God. Rather, in realizing that he would not be accepted as the Messiah by the Jewish nation, Jesus took the only course available to him. He "resolved to take the cross as the condition of indemnity to pay for the accomplishment of the spiritual salvation of man" when he discovered he could not accomplish both the spiritual and the physical salvation (DP 151).

If Jesus had not been crucified, then he would have found the perfect mate and founded God's perfect family on earth, thus accomplishing both the physical and the spiritual salvation. As it was, "his body was invaded by Satan, and he was killed. . . . In this manner, however devout a man of faith may be, he cannot fulfill physical salvation by redemption through Jesus' crucifixion alone" (DP 147-48).

Moreover, according to the *Divine Principle,* Jesus did not appear in bodily form after his physical death and before his ascension. Rather, he was "a being transcendent of time and space" (DP 360) and appeared to his disciples as a spirit being.

It is obvious that this understanding of Jesus and God raises questions concerning the traditional notion of Trinity. The *Divine Principle* essentially rejects this doctrine, arguing, for example, that when in the Bible God speaks in the plural he is not speaking from the standpoint of a "trinity" but as the head over the angels (DP 76). Jesus, who according to traditional understanding of passages such as John 1:1-3 took an active part in the creation of the universe, is seen by the *Divine Principle* as taking part in creation only in the sense that all perfected men do so because of their fulfillment of the purpose of creation (DP 211). Finally, the doctrine of God is put in terms of the male/female doctrine of creation: "There must be a True Mother with a True Father, in order to give rebirth to fallen children as children of goodness. She is the Holy Spirit" (DP 215).

The divinity of Jesus, therefore, is limited to his being a "perfected man." Thus he may be said "to even possess deity" (DP 209), and in light of this, "he may well be called God. Nevertheless, he can by no means be God himself" (DP 210-11). While he was on earth, Jesus was no different from any other person "except for the fact that he was without original sin" (DP 212).

In summary, Jesus saved man *spiritually* but not *physically* because he was crucified by the Jews and because he was unable to meet his perfect mate and establish the Kingdom of Heaven on earth. Therefore the Messiah or Lord of the Second Advent must come to complete God's goal for creation.

The Lord of the Second Advent. It is necessary here to emphasize that the goal of creation to perfect man spiritually requires the process to be accomplished through physical life on earth. There is essentially no difference between a Christian, no matter how devout, and an Old Testament saint; neither have been able to get rid of original sin or to "remove themselves from the lineage of Satan." The Lord of the Second Advent "must be born on earth, in flesh," in order to accomplish man's physical salvation (DP 368-369).

The *Divine Principle* devotes a major portion of its study to numerology. The number 2,000 provides the key to the coming of the Lord of the Second Advent. The *Divine Principle* states that Jesus came 2,000 years after Abraham, during which time God had prepared the first coming of the Messiah (DP 499). Therefore, the Lord of the Second Advent will come 2,000 years after Jesus, during which time God has prepared the second coming of the Messiah. It may be concluded from this that the Messiah may be coming at any moment, if he has not already arrived.

The *Divine Principle* not only dates the Second Advent but indicates the birthplace as well. Basing its case on Revelation 7:2-4, which describes "another angel ascending from the rising of the sun, having the seal of the living God," the *Divine Principle* concludes that Christ will be born in a country in the East. This, it continues, has meant "from ancient times" the nations of Korea, Japan and China (DP 519-520).

The *Divine Principle* examines each of the three countries as possibilities for the birthplace. It notes that Japan is a nation which has worshiped Amaterasuomikami and has entered the period of the Second Advent as a totalitarian nation that has persecuted

Christians in Korea. China as a communist nation is on the Satanic side. The *Divine Principle* therefore concludes that the Lord of the Second Advent will be born in Korea (DP 520).

We might expect the *Divine Principle* to state that Sun Myung Moon is the Lord of the Second Advent. It does not. Neither the *Divine Principle* nor Moon himself will declare publicly today that he is the Messiah, nor will a majority of his followers. There are a good many reasons for this, but proselytizing is the strongest. Moon's followers believe that potential converts will react negatively to their doctrine of the second coming, if presented at initial confrontations. They further believe that those who hear and reject the revelations given to Moon by God will be condemned. Therefore, their desire and effort is to gather the lost under their loving wings and then introduce the doctrine of the *Divine Principle*. Each convert can then decide within his own heart who the Lord of the Second Advent is.

In summary, people of all faiths would have accepted Jesus as the Messiah but for his death. The Lord of the Second Advent now takes Jesus' place and all religions will unite under him. In fact, everyone who is conscientious will accept the Lord of the Second Advent (DP 189-190).

A Warning to Christians. Although inviting people of other faiths and beliefs, the *Divine Principle* concludes with a warning to Christians. It claims that Christians today will be like the priests and rabbis of Jesus' day, the "first to persecute the Messiah" (DP 533). The warning is ominous: "Innumerable Christians of today are dashing on the way which they think will lead them to the Kingdom of Heaven. Nevertheless, this very road is apt to lead them into hell" (DP 535).

Such a warning puts Christians in the awkward position of being critics of the truth. We will soon see if this is a fair appraisal.

A Biblical Critique
A biblical critique of the *Divine Principle*'s contention is dealt a severe blow if one believes that the Bible is not absolute truth. If

the Bible is set aside, by what standard can the *Divine Principle* be compared, contrasted and refuted?[6]

Indeed, the question of authority is the main issue in dealing with the Moon doctrine, as it is in dealing with any religious teaching. For a Christian there can be only one basic authority on matters concerning God and our relationship to him—the Bible and the Bible alone. For lack of space, I can only assume this position here. Readers who wish to investigate the authority of Scripture are encouraged to read John R. W. Stott's brief booklet *The Authority of the Bible* or John Wenham's extended analysis in *Christ and the Bible*.[7]

In any case, it is important to note that the apostle Paul predicted the sort of skepticism found in the Moon doctrine. "All Scripture is inspired by God" (2 Tim 3:16), he wrote to Timothy, and then he commented, "The time is coming when people will not endure sound teaching, but having itching ears they will accumulate for themselves teachers to suit their own likings, and will turn away from listening to the truth and wander into myths" (2 Tim 4:3-4).

The First Adam. One of the most incredible myths is the *Divine Principle*'s account of the fall of Adam and Eve. The plain story of Genesis 3 is abandoned and replaced with an allegorical account which begins by declaring the tree of life to be the symbol of perfected Adam and the tree of knowledge to be the symbol of Eve. It is here that the *Divine Principle* begins to introduce concepts that are alien to the Bible.

As difficult as it is to understand how Satan could tempt Eve with the fruit of herself, it takes an even greater leap of faith to accept this faulty reasoning: It is the nature of man to cover the area of transgression; Adam and Eve covered the sexual areas of their bodies; therefore they committed sexual sin and it is that sin which constitutes the fall.

Where and how does one learn that it is the nature of man to cover the area of transgression? This is clearly an extrabiblical principle which one needs to accept before the argument can proceed. It has no warrant either in the Bible or in experience. Does a child who has just hit his baby brother hide his hand when the baby cries?

Second, the notion that Eve had sexual contact with Satan has no biblical support whatsoever. Nor is there warrant in either the Old or New Testament for an interpretation of the fall along the *spiritual* and *physical* lines suggested in the *Divine Principle*. To accept the *Divine Principle* as a theological basis, one must place faith in Sun Myung Moon himself and in the revelation he claims to have been given. Traditionally, the fall has been understood by Christians to consist of Adam and Eve's disobedience of a direct command of God not to eat the fruit of the tree of the knowledge of good and evil. It is clear from 1 Timothy 2:14 that Adam knew what he was doing when he disobeyed. It is Adam's rebellion, his direct disobedience, which constitutes the fall.

The reason that Adam and Eve hid from God and sewed garments to cover their nakedness is that they felt ashamed and guilty. They wanted to avoid a confrontation with God. It is not that their nakedness or their sexual parts constituted sin, for all of God's creation, including the sexual ("male and female" in Genesis 1:27) was declared good prior to the fall. Therefore, when they covered themselves they were demonstrating an unhealthy and inaccurate awareness of who they themselves were. They were now seeing things from Satan's point of view.

It is questionable whether the *Divine Principle* leaves room for man's responsibility, as does the traditional understanding of the fall. If Eve was seduced by Satan and then in turn seduced Adam, were not both of them victims of Satan's nefarious desires rather than agents responsible for their own actions? That would suggest that God did not make Adam and Eve capable of withstanding temptation from Satan. That places the responsibility for sin squarely at the feet of God. The Bible, however, does not do this.

Another point of discord between the Bible and the *Divine Principle* is the notion that Cain is the fruit of Eve's relation with Satan. Genesis 4:1 says, "Now the man had relations with his wife

Eve, and she conceived and gave birth to Cain." The *Divine Principle* does not merely read into the Scriptures additional material but misrepresents what is clearly stated.

The Second Adam. Further distortion of Scriptures is readily discerned in the *Divine Principle*'s reference to Christ as the second Adam. Paul said to the Corinthians: "Thus it is written, 'The first man Adam became a living being'; the last Adam became a life-giving spirit" (1 Cor 15:45). The followers of the Unification Church believe that "the last Adam" is the Lord of the Second Advent, but it is clear from verse 47 that he could only be Jesus Christ.

As we saw, the *Divine Principle* argues that Jesus did not fulfill God's plan of total redemption. This was due to the Jews' failure to believe in Jesus because of John the Baptist. The apostle John, however, said, "And many came to him; and they said, 'John did no sign, but everything that John said about this man was true.' And many believed in him there" (Jn 10:41-42).

Throughout his ministry, John the Baptist pointed to Jesus as the Messiah, even directing some of the apostles to him. If anything, John opened the eyes of the Jews to the coming of the Messiah. Nevertheless, followers of the Unification Church argue that all the flattering references to John were made by those writers who had a limited understanding of the spiritual significance of John's actions. Yet, late in his ministry and long after John had been beheaded, Jesus himself said, "For John came to you in the way of righteousness" (Mt 21:32).

It is at this point that the *Divine Principle* contends that Jesus had to take the way of the cross, which was one of two paths prophesied by the prophets. If the Jews had believed in him, Jesus would have taken the path leading to the establishment of the Kingdom of Heaven on earth. Jesus could then have redeemed people physically and forgiven them spiritually.

The Bible tells a different story. In Matthew 5:17-18 Jesus said, "Think not that I have come to abolish the law and the prophets; I have come not to abolish them but to fulfill them. For truly, I say

164

to you, till heaven and earth pass away, not an iota, not a dot, or stroke shall pass away from the Law, until all is accomplished." In other words, all prophecy is to be accomplished. This, of course, conflicts with the *Divine Principle*'s position which requires that the prophecy of the death of Christ (Isaiah 53 and Psalm 22) not be fulfilled if the Jews accept Jesus as the Messiah.

Concerning the physical resurrection of Christ, the *Divine Principle* employs two passages to support its claim that Jesus "was a being transcendent of time and space" (DP 360). One incident occurs when "the doors were shut, but Jesus came and stood among them" (Jn 20:26). The *Divine Principle* reasons that Jesus could not have been physical if the doors were shut. The next verse, however, dispels that deduction: "Then he said to Thomas, 'Put your finger here, and see my hands; and put out your hand, and place it in my side; do not be faithless, but believing.''

The second incident occurs when Jesus walked with his disciples who did not recognize him. The crucial verse is Luke 24:31: "And their eyes were opened and they recognized him; and he vanished out of their sight." The language can be read in their favor or as a colorful description of the incident. The following verses, however, settle any dispute over Christ's physical resurrection:

As they were saying this, Jesus himself stood among them. But they were startled and frightened, and supposed that they saw a spirit. And he said to them, "Why are you troubled, and why do questionings rise in your hearts? See my hands and my feet, that it is I myself; handle me, and see; for a spirit has not flesh and bones as you see that I have." And while they still disbelieved for joy, and wondered, he said to them, "Have you anything here to eat?" They gave him a piece of broiled fish; and he took it and ate it before them. (Lk 24:36-43)

Finally, we should note Moon's teaching about the Trinity. There are two major discrepancies between the *Divine Principle* and Jesus' words at the Last Supper. In reference to the Holy Spirit as "a True Mother," the *Divine Principle* is in obvious conflict with John 14:26; 15:26; 16:7, where Jesus referred to the Holy

Spirit in the third person masculine.

There is a second point of conflict: Jesus further said at the Last Supper, "And now, Father, glorify thou me in thy own presence with the glory which I had with thee before the world was made" (Jn 17:5). Here Jesus himself claims that he was not part of creation but with the Father from the beginning.

It is true that Jesus never said, "I am God." Consequently the *Divine Principle* has little trouble in twisting into its own line of reasoning the verses substantiating Jesus' divinity. Such verses as "I am in my Father" (Jn 14:20) are juxtaposed with such verses as "My God, My God, why hast thou forsaken me?" (Mt 27:46) to prove that Jesus is not God; for how could he forsake himself? Certainly Jesus is not the Father, but it does not follow that, because he is not the Father, he does not possess full deity. Rather, Paul said to the Colossians, "For in him the whole fulness of deity dwells bodily, and you have come to fulness of life in him, who is the head of all rule and authority" (Col 2:9-10). Again the *Divine Principle* has misinterpreted the biblical data.

The Lord of the Second Advent. With regard to the Lord of the Second Advent, the primary area of disagreement is that the Bible prophesies the return of Jesus Christ not as a baby, as with Jesus' first coming, but as the risen Lord coming on the clouds of the sky (Mt 24:30). Christ will come to reign and to judge. Jesus the Savior has already been born, not in the East but in Bethlehem. When he comes again it will be in the manner the disciples saw him go (Acts 1:11).

Nonetheless, as to when the Messiah will come again, the *Divine Principle* may be correct in asserting that he will return in this present age. The Bible indicates that God alone knows the time. Jesus said plainly, "Of that day and hour no one knows, not even the angels of heaven, nor the Son, but the Father only" (Mt 24:36). If Moon is right, therefore, it is only by accident.

As to the location of the origin of the Lord of the Second Advent, the *Divine Principle* ties together an incredible string of assertions. First, it asserts that "another angel" is the Messiah and not an actual angel. Second, it asserts that "from the rising of the sun" is from the East and not from an eastward direction. Third, it asserts that the East refers to the Orient and not a more likely location such as the Middle East. Fourth, it asserts that the East refers to Korea, Japan and China and not any other Oriental nation. Finally, it asserts that Korea is the birthplace of the Messiah. Why not claim Japan as the place referred to since it calls itself the place of "the rising sun"? To accept Korea as the birthplace is to rest the maximum of faith upon the minimum of logic.

Nonetheless, despite these weaknesses in Moon's teachings, despite their incompatibility with either the Bible or secular thought, many young people are turning to the Unification Church. We need to know why.

Conversion to the Moon Doctrine

"I truly disciplined and set the traditions of our movement in Korea, so that they [those in the movement] were completely liberated from the fear of how to live, what to eat, and how to sleep."[8] These are the words of Sun Myung Moon. They raise the controversial question: What induces the followers of Moon to accept his doctrine wholeheartedly? Is it a technique like brainwashing, mind-control, mind manipulation, behavior modification? Or is it heavenly indoctrination or simply total faith in Moon and his ideas? An overview of a person's encounter with, acceptance of and life in the Unification Church or its many front organizations may help us discover why so many young people have chosen a lifestyle which seems incredible to so many others.

The Encounter. The followers of Moon you are most likely to meet are young people, a majority of whom are in their twenties. They are well-groomed and polite. They dress simply and wear little or no make-up. Young men with short hair and young women in neat, modest skirts and dresses give a clean-cut, conservative image. Their most striking characteristic is their smiles. That is a key to winning you to their movement.

Although most of their proselytizing takes place on college campuses, you may find them at shopping centers, libraries, airports or wherever a mass of people congregates. Their primary aim is to persuade you to accept an invitation to their center for dinner.

They may employ one of a number of lines of persuasion, depending upon your beliefs and personality. Generally anything you are into, they will say they are into. Their common line is that they are in a movement which is unifying the peoples of all races and beliefs around love and fraternity. They invite you to their center where you can see different people with many backgrounds and from different cultures demonstrate their love and where you can hear how they hope to achieve this goal.

If you fail to accept their invitation, then their secondary aim is to obtain your name and phone number. Later they may telephone you as much as three to five times a day for a month. Some people go just to stop their calling.

When you attend their dinners, you are again met with smiles. Two sets of people are present: the followers of Moon and those who have been invited like yourself. Among the followers, there are those who circulate among the guests and those who are assigned to a specific guest. You are often complimented on your looks, personality, dress or whatever. Most important, they want to impress upon you that they love you.

Along with the meal, you are introduced to a speaker who gives a set lecture about the problems and needs of the world and how they are building a community based on universal love. Moon is rarely mentioned to anyone at the first encounter or here at the dinner.

While you eat with them, listen to their lectures and prayers, and share in their singing, you again notice their constant smiles. You also wonder why they never give you an opportunity to withdraw and reflect upon what is happening. The former is making a deep impression on you; the latter you pass off as their concern for you.

Finally they ask you to attend a workshop. These last 3, 7, 21 or 120 days, but the first one to which they normally invite you is the three-day workshop. Depending on the area of the country, the workshop may be located at a church, an estate, a camp, a training center or a rural retreat. In any case, their invitation is extremely alluring.

The Workshop. By the time you reach their workshop, you will realize that the followers of Moon regard each other as "family." Soon you will also realize that you are spoken of as a "spiritual child," the youngest member of a tightly knit family, each with his own specific role.

It becomes immediately apparent to you that you are not to be left alone and that all "spiritual children" have someone of the opposite sex from the family assigned to them. If you should wander off by yourself, someone will follow you and politely ask you to rejoin the group.

You also learn that there is a rigidly held schedule. There are specific times for eating, exercising, playing, singing, listening to lectures and discussing them. You are separated into small groups led by a team leader who has to have perfect control. Rarely are you permitted to engage in casual conversation with anyone. Creativity is taunted and you see only conformity.

All day you are bombarded by ideas. There is little relaxation, and so your resistance is low. When you refrain from sharing or resist in any way, you are met with benevolent concern. Peer approval is an important technique which subtly tells you to conform. The family members aim directly at your most vulnerable points: the need to belong, to feel useful and to feel loved. Throughout the workshop you are flooded with affection—hugs, pats, hand-holding and smiles.

There comes a point when negative reaction to the regimental control gives way to automatic reaction. You then try to please, but the only way is to conform. Furthermore, your intellectual objection is being undercut by means of emotional seduction. You succumb many times to small acts of conformity without realizing it. You feel guilty when you hold back, and you are told that wanting to be alone is a symptom of fear and alienation. You also note that the lectures are becoming more emotional and that you are being infected by them.

It is at this point that you are asked to join their movement. The family member who has been with you the most will beg and plead with you to stay. There will even be tears along with the promises. They will continue to implore until you decide to stay.

The Indoctrination. After you have committed yourself to the movement, things will begin to change; but first, they give you about two weeks of adjustment. During this time, you are expected to give all your possessions to the movement. Furthermore, the church sees to it that being with them makes you so vulnerable and so unable to cope with the real world that you are compelled to stay with them. You are taught that everyone not in the movement is under the influence of Satan and that you should mistrust them. The devil works strongest through those closest to you, they insist. This naturally offsets the concern of parents and friends. Thus you become dependent on the group for love and positive reinforcement. After alienation is complete, you are told that you can leave if you want.

By now you will have been familiarized with Moon, his doctrine and his movement. You speak of him as Master or Father. Through him God has imparted revelations revealed in the *Divine Principle* and his sermons. Moon and his wife are the Perfect Parents who will bring physical salvation to you and the world. To you Moon is everything.

You are also required to adhere to a schedule more demanding than the workshop's. You sleep five or six hours a day. Your diet consists of starchy foods, low in proteins. Often you must fast for many days. You are continually praying and studying the *Principle.* You are out for long hours in all weather conditions, asking for donations or selling flowers and candy any way you can. And you are taught that because Satan deceives God's children, you are justified in deceiving Satan's children, a doctrine known as "heavenly deception."

If your body reacts negatively with illness or fatigue, it is a sign of Satan invading your body. If you begin to work less, they say you are being selfish and not growing close to God. If you object to their rules, they say it is Satan working through you against God. You are taught to mistrust your mind. You are given an interpretation for every situation. You no longer need to think or evaluate for yourself but instead recall what was told you for that situation. If you leave, they say, you will die spiritually and be possessed by Satan physically.

You become so dependent that you will do anything for them and Moon.

Recruiting. Daily life in a house is a totally regulated training process designed to lead each individual to the perfect state, to provide monetary support for the movement and to win converts. You achieve perfection in a period of about three years. In order to become perfect, you must receive Moon's blessing. To do so you must bring three "spiritual children" into the church. When perfection is attained, you are entitled to marry a perfect mate chosen by the movement. It is extremely important for you to marry because marriage is essential for your complete salvation.

Consequently you search the streets for potential converts. You are told that the college campuses are especially ripe with vulnerable people during final exams. You are told that dead churches also have many vulnerable people; reaching them is called "infiltration." You are eager to invite people to the center, and your face wears a big smile.

Responding to Followers of Moon
When you first encounter a follower of Moon, you may think you are looking at yourself. You see someone whose needs are like yours but who seems to be fulfilled, and in your own weakness you may be led astray. The only security from this trap is Jesus. By truly knowing him, having a right relationship with him and loving him, you will not be vulnerable to your supposed mirror image. Then, instead of their sharing Moon and his doctrine with you, you can share Jesus with them.

A sacred aphorism of the Buddha is that "the moon makes the night beautiful." Although the Buddha didn't mean it in this way,

Sun Myung Moon has made the spiritual forces of darkness appear beautiful to thousands of young people. One mission of Christ's church is to challenge the Moon doctrine and to uphold the gospel of Christ in love and in truth.

Paul warned the Christians against such teaching as the Moon doctrine: "See to it that no one makes a prey of you by philosophy and empty deceit, according to human tradition, according to the elemental spirits of the universe, and not according to Christ (Col 2:8).

Today we are barraged by many doctrines claiming to be the way to God. Many religious leaders and spiritual masters proclaim that they alone have the truth. How is one to really know whom to believe? Christians claim that if the testimony of Jesus' words is established in any man's heart, he need go no further than John 14:6. Jesus said, "I am the way, and the truth, and the life; no one comes to the Father, but by me."[9]

11
The Way
Joel A. MacCollam

*The Word means what it says, and it
says what it means.*
Victor Paul Wierwille

YOU CAN HAVE POWER FOR Abundant Living." "Learn how to
kick the fear and worry habit . . . how to understand this crazy,
mixed-up world and what the Bible says about it . . . how to separate truth from baloney . . . how to knock the devil right in the old
schnazola . . . how Jesus Christ fits into all of this." So promise
posters on college bulletin boards around the United States.

Claiming to teach "keys to understanding the most exciting
HOW TO DO IT BOOK ever written,"[1] The Way International and
its recently retired president, Victor Paul Wierwille, have been
attracting increased interest from many sources. And The Way's
new leadership team under the Reverend Craig Martindale promises more of the same.

Young people are interested because of the experiential emphasis of The Way's spirituality. Some parents are alarmed because

The Way allegedly is helping to subvert the foundation of the American family. Psychologists are concerned about the changes in personality which many Way people exhibit and how those changes were made. Theologians often question the historical accuracy and scholarly honesty of The Way's teachings.

What is The Way? Who is Victor Paul Wierwille? What are his teachings? What are we to make of this new religious phenomenon?

In its own literature, The Way is described as a "biblical research and teaching organization concerned with setting before men and women . . . the inherent accuracy of the Word of God. . . . The Way is not a church, nor is it a denomination or a religious sect of any sort."[2] (Still, the movement enjoys tax-exempt status with the Internal Revenue Service as a nonprofit organization, and Way ministers are accepted as ordained clergy in many states and in many places are licensed to perform marriages.)

Estimates of adherents to The Way vary from twenty thousand to one hundred thousand. Followers are tightly organized on the model of a tree. The tree's trunk is the International Headquarters at New Knoxville, Ohio. The board of directors is the root; the state organization is the limb; city-wide or regional ministries are the branches; the local fellowship in a home or on campus is the twig; and each Way believer is a leaf. The Way places its strongest emphasis at the twig level, and it is here that the group's theological exclusiveness coupled with strong peer pressure to "band together" in worship and fellowship, as well as the accepted status of Way ministers as ordained clergy, combine to suggest that The Way does indeed function as a church. "Like a tree, the 'life' of the ministry is in the twig (where the leaves cluster) where the accuracy of God's Word is taught oftentimes daily, as during the first-century church. It is here in the twig that each believer becomes 'rooted and grounded and established' in his knowledge and practical application of The Word."[3]

Along with their professed spiritual goals to put "the Word over the World" (the WOW program), The Way clearly seeks new followers. While the initial "Power for Abundant Living" (PFAL) course has been offered for as much as $200 (including all course books), the current $40 registration fee (which excludes many of the more expensive books needed) appears to be a shrewd marketing technique designed both to make the course more initially attractive and to reduce criticism from nonfollowers. Through aggressive evangelism The Way Corps (a further responsibility after joining) has set a goal of 3,220,000 students in its ranks by 1990.[4]

Victor Paul Wierwille

Who is the founder of this well-organized and ambitious group? Tanned and well-dressed, with Holy Spirit doves on his cufflinks, tieclasp, lapel pin and ring, Victor Paul Wierwille is an impressive figure. His smile is infectious and attractive. Once content to visit Way members around the country on his Harley-Davidson motorcycle, he now uses an elaborately converted bus (which carries his personal research library for biblical studies at all times) and a private airplane for his travels. And this equipment will not lie idle during his retirement; Wierwille still will travel and preach extensively for the movement he has founded.

Raised in a strict fundamentalist atmosphere, Wierwille prepared for the ministry at the University of Chicago Divinity School and Princeton Seminary (where he received a master's degree). "The Doctor," as many followers call him, received his honorary doctorate from Pike's Peak Seminary, "a reputed degree mill."[5]

The early years of his ministry were spent in the Evangelical and Reformed Church. While he was pastor of St. Peter's Church in Van Wert, Ohio, however, the denomination authorized appointment of a committee "to bring forth recommendations for action" about his ministry.[6] A short while later, on May 23, 1958, Wierwille resigned and The Way started to grow.

His theological differences with the Evangelical and Reformed Church were rooted in his earlier decision to burn his theological library and set an independent path for discovering the meaning of Scripture. By 1953, well before his resignation, he had established the "Power for Abundant Living" course. In 1958 this product of his independent research became the cornerstone of The Way International.

Wierwille describes his encounter with God: "I was praying . . . and that's when He spoke to me audibly, just like I'm talking to you now. He said He would teach me the Word as it has not been known since the first century if I would teach it to others."[7]

Wierwille's writing and preaching commitments are hectic and he seems to consider his work an apostolic ministry. He defines an apostle as "one who brings new light to his generation."

Unfortunately for Wierwille, his definition means he flunks his own test. Many of the theological thoughts he has espoused are derived, without adequate credit, from the works of E. W. Bullinger. Even more serious, Wierwille lifted numerous and substantial direct quotations from Bullinger's *The Giver and His Gifts* and *How to Enjoy the Bible* without giving any credit or mention to the original author. In much of Wierwille's work there is no "new light to [this] generation," only a reflection of another's efforts.

Joining The Way

The "others"—The Way adherents—come mostly from middle-class backgrounds. The majority are between eighteen and twenty-four, though some older people are involved. A large Way gathering presents a clean-cut appearance—few "hippy" types are present. Conference organizers are well-dressed young men in fashionable three-piece suits, wearing highly polished shoes and carrying leather attaché cases.

The primary recruitment emphasis of The Way is directed at college campuses. Twig leaders stress personal contact between believers and potential converts. Many former Way people tell of being approached by a friendly individual who presented a strongly visible "Christian" image while showing a high degree of personal interest in the potential convert.

This personal approach is developed through "Witnessing and

Undershepherding," which is both an advanced seminar for Way believers and an essential element of recruiting. The Way actively trains people to develop prospects for the PFAL class: "Remember, you are not selling anything door to door. The hungry ones will come to the twig to register for the class (PFAL)."[8]

Undershepherding is described as "watching over, not taking over" and appears to be genuine friendship. Way believers are encouraged, for example, to reinforce a person's good points through compliments, to do "little things for him," and "to schedule your person into your life."

While this sounds quite wholesome, former Way members and some parents of current believers feel that some recruitment techniques have the potential for creating severe personality disorientation. One former Way follower experienced the friendly concern but now feels that gradually his mind was manipulated.

He reports that life in The Way was "exercise, going to work, and fellowship." This lifestyle also featured only four hours of sleep a night. This cycle of exercise, work and fellowship led him to physical and mental exhaustion. "When you are at this point is when they really get heavy and start coming down on you, reading scriptures to you, explaining to you what they mean. You are at the point where you are so physically and mentally fatigued that you take exactly what they say for granted. You get to the point where you are so involved . . . you are so brainwashed, that anything they tell you, you are going to believe. It took The Way ministry about one month to accomplish this."[9]

The Way has also used their style of friendship evangelism in "skimming," where articulate followers of Martindale and Wierwille visit churches (usually evangelical) and invite new converts to their "Bible studies" (actually "twig" meetings). In one large southern California congregation, Way people actually came forward for altar calls and recruited prospective followers immediately after the close of the service. Several from The Way have also enrolled at major conservative or evangelical Christian Bible schools and seminaries to work these new "mission fields."

Fear of Satan is emphasized strongly during indoctrination. The Way's belief that everything apart from their work is "natural man" and therefore subject to the influence of the devil causes many to elect to stay close to the twig fellowship. A former leaf said, "The point came where I was so deathly afraid of the devil, of Satan, that the only way I could deal with him was to keep going to twig meetings."[10]

No matter how many twig meetings a convert attends, the accepted sign of "believing" is in taking the PFAL course. For a $40 "donation" plus the cost of several textbooks, the student is allowed to sit for twelve three-hour taped sessions of teachings by Wierwille. Note-taking is forbidden, and "there is no time for questioning until the final session."[11] The highlight of PFAL occurs when "The Doctor" teaches his students how to speak in tongues as an essential part of the more abundant life he offers.

The Way makes no apology for the "donation" (which is really tuition) required for the introductory course. The receipts from PFAL go directly to The Way's national headquarters to "further the ministry." (Posters proclaiming the benefits of PFAL draw as many as one thousand registrations a month.) A convert's ability to produce the required donation is taken as a sign of "right believing." Anyone who desires to take the PFAL and is unable to produce the needed funds is not believing strongly enough and is refused admission to the course which promises great spiritual benefits.

Once the initial steps for membership are accomplished (witnessing and undershepherding, twig fellowship and PFAL), The Way's world is open: The Way Corps, work at Headquarters, twig leadership, music ministry, the WOW program and numerous other expressions of Wierwille's vision. Way leaders committed three million dollars to the purchase and renovation of a college campus in Kansas where The Way offers an unaccredited program of Bible study, as well as weapons training and other survival skills. Wierwille's son, Donald, a former elementary school principal, is dean of The Way College of Emporia. Also The Way has its own publishing house, The American Christian Press, which specializes in *The Way Magazine,* a teaching and news bimonthly, and Dr. Wierwille's many books and tracts.

The Way also espouses a strongly conservative political viewpoint, and Wierwille has consistently encouraged his people to support the Constitutional Political Alliance (CPA, formerly the Christian Political Alliance). Led for several years by Hayes Gahagan, a former state senator from Maine and strong Way supporter, CPA applied The Way's theological methodology to constitutional principles, encouraging "believers" to "rightly divide the Constitution" just as Way believers are urged to "rightly divide the Word." Although CPA has been a factor in The Way's overall structure in the past, it has not been visible to the public in recent months, nor has it been mentioned in either *The Way Magazine* or the *Grapevine,* the group's monthly newsletter.

The Total Fitness Institute, a Way operation in North Fork, California, aims "to help believers discover and experience more about walking with the Father."[12] But a California educational official apparently does not understand the religious nature of TFI. He writes: "This school teaches survival skills only. This school *has an affiliation with the California State University* at Fresno for enrollment for college credit"[13] (emphasis added). TFI's survival principles have also been taught at a Way ranch near Farmington, New Mexico.

Not limiting his group to the American religious marketplace, Wierwille has led The Way into a truly international outreach, focusing particularly on South America and Europe; an extensive tour of South America was completed in 1982, and Europe is targeted for further ministry expansion.

Problems in Way Theology

Victor Paul Wierwille's interpretations of Scripture form the foundation for The Way's theology. "The Doctor" has two reasons for using the Bible for his theology. First, he believes strongly that through The Way's ministry God is revealing insights hidden since the time of St. Paul. The second reason is grounded on Wierwille's understanding of Scripture: "The Word says what it means, and it means what it says." There is no room for interpretation or discussion. "We must come to The Word, let The Word speak, and then adjust our thinking according to the integrity and accuracy of The Word. After we have let The Word speak, we must accordingly harmonize our beliefs, our actions, and our living."[14]

And according to Wierwille, what does the Word say? Let him speak for himself: "You show me one place in the Bible where it says He [Jesus] is God. . . . I don't want you rapping, your doubletalk, your tripletalk; all I want is Scripture."[15] The primary error in Wierwille's theology is his denial of the deity of Jesus Christ. The doctrinal problem is common to many of the cultic offshoots of orthodox Christianity. Wierwille writes: "The Bible teaches that there is only one true God, that God was in Christ, that God is Spirit, and that God is eternal whereas Jesus was born."[16] "Jesus Christ's existence began when He was conceived by God's creating the soul-life of Jesus in Mary."[17]

Rejection of the Trinity. Though Wierwille starts with a statement that sounds relatively orthodox to a Christian ("there is only one true God"), he means something quite different by it. He understands God to be a single person (unitarian monotheism) while orthodox Christianity holds that there is one God in three persons (trinitarian monotheism). Wierwille's rejection of the Trinity is based on his prior rejection of the deity of Jesus Christ and the distinct personhood of the Holy Spirit. We shall examine each in turn.

There is a hint of the plurality within God's oneness even in the central confession of Judaism: "Hear, O Israel: The LORD our God is one LORD" (Deut 6:4; Mk 12:29). The Hebrew word *echoid* ("one") does not suggest the absolute oneness which Wierwille implies. *Echoid* is used in Genesis 2:24 where it indicates a composite oneness: "they become one flesh." Obviously, *echoid* here does not mean that the man and the woman become one single person. No, their bodies, souls and spirits still maintain individual characteristics.

Wierwille also fails to understand the significance of the Hebrew word for God. *Elohim* is a plural noun which is used with a singular verb and may be used to indicate composite oneness. And in Genesis 1:26 God said, "Let us make man in our image, after our likeness," suggesting plurality of person. Wierwille attempts to explain away this translation in a confusing and unscholarly comparison with English culture and usage of the royal "we."[18]

Furthermore, there is much Old Testament evidence to support the pre-existence and deity of Jesus Christ. For example, the prophet Micah, hundreds of years before Christ, spoke of Jesus in these words: "From you [Judah] shall come forth for me one who is to be ruler in Israel, whose origin is from of old, from ancient days" (5:2). Wierwille acknowledges the gift of prophecy, but he passes by this Old Testament prophecy (only one of many) because it does not fit into his scholarship.

Rejection of Jesus' Deity. In his book entitled *Jesus Christ Is Not God,* Wierwille explicitly denies Jesus' deity. For The Way, Jesus Christ is important, but the Father alone is God; Jesus is the Son of God, but he is not God the Son.

While Wierwille claims to teach the "rightly divided" Word as it has not been known since the first century, his own teachings concerning the deity of Christ are only a rendition of a doctrine popular in the third century. When Paul of Samasota, Bishop of Antioch from 260 to 272, taught this doctrine, it was branded as heresy and called "Monarchianism."[19]

But Jesus himself claimed equality with the Father: "I and the Father are one" (Jn 10:30). On this statement Wierwille comments, "It has already been established that Jesus and God are not one from the beginning, but they were one in purpose as shown in the context of this verse as Jesus declared his Father on earth. God and Jesus Christ's unanimity of purpose is poignantly shown in that Jesus Christ always did the Father's will and finished the work for which God had sent him."[20]

While Jesus' declaration certainly indicates a unity of purpose, we cannot limit the implication of his statement to that one condition. If Jesus had meant only that he and the Father were one in purpose, the strong reaction which the remark elicited would never have occurred. Why would the Jews try to stone someone for adhering to a principle they would admire, namely, being godlike in deeds and actions (Jn 10:31-39)? No, the Jews were outraged because Jesus claimed an *essential* unity (the composite unity mentioned earlier) with the Father. If we hold (as both orthodox Christianity and The Way agree) that Jesus was a man without sin, then he would not have lied. It was Jesus' truthful assertion of divinity which inflamed the Jews.

Even if Wierwille's qualified acceptance and limited application of the Old Testament and the Gospels were valid, there is still an abundance of evidence for Christ's pre-existence in the Epistles which Wierwille stresses so much. Paul's description of Christ, for example, could hardly be said of even the most exceptional man; it is a description of deity: "He [the Father] has delivered us from the dominion of darkness and transferred us to the kingdom of his beloved Son, in whom we have redemption, the forgiveness of sins. He [the Son] is the image of the invisible God, the first-born of all creation; . . . all things were created through him and for him. He is before all things, and in him all things hold together. He is the head of the body, the church; . . . that in everything he might be pre-eminent. For in him all the fulness of God was pleased to dwell" (Col 1:13-19). Jesus Christ, the one by whom and for whom all things were created, also took on flesh and entered that creation.

Mistranslation of John 1. Wierwille's treatment of John 1:1-18, one of the principal texts on the Incarnation of the Word of God, deserves special attention. In contrast to John's explicit proclamation of Christ's true deity and true humanity and the unity of his person, Wierwille directly challenges the authority of these verses by making his own unique additions and interpretations. His exegesis of this passage is based on the presupposition that "the Bible teaches that there is only one true God, that God was in Christ, that God is Spirit, and that God is eternal in contrast to Jesus whose beginning was his birth."[21] He asserts that the Word (Jesus) was not "in the beginning" with God as a part of the Godhead, as is maintained by orthodox interpretation of John 1:1: "In the beginning was the Word, and the Word was with God, and the Word was God." Instead Wierwille says the Word was pre-existent with the Father only in his foreknowledge. "When Jesus was born, he came into existence.... Foreknowledge became a reality."[22]

Without regard to the original, early manuscripts available for research, Wierwille adds the word *revealed* to his "literal" translation of John 1:1: "In the beginning (before the creation) God was the Word, and the revealed Word was in God's foreknowledge."[23] In John's first phrase, the Word is identified with God. In order to avoid the implication of this (that is, that the incarnate Word— Jesus Christ—is one in identity with the Father), Wierwille inserts a word into the text *(revealed)* which suggests that a distinction exists between the "Word" that *was* God and the "revealed Word" that was merely *with* God *in his foreknowledge*. In this way he escapes the otherwise unavoidable conclusion that this passage teaches the oneness of the Word (Jesus Christ) and God (see Jn 1:14-17).

Wierwille continues this strategy into verse 2, translating it: "The revealed word was in the beginning with God."[24] Once again *revealed* is his own additon to the text.

In verse 3, Wierwille changes the phrase "all things were made by him" (the Word of verses 1 and 2) to "all things were made by God." He justifies this change on the grounds that "only God was in the beginning as stated in Genesis 1:1."[25] This is supposed to mean that *only* God (as over against God in company with the Word and the Spirit) was in the beginning. But Genesis 1:1 is simply telling us exactly what God did in the beginning, and John 1:1-3 means that the Word (Jesus Christ) was in the beginning with God participating in the creation of all things.

Furthermore, without textual justification Wierwille stresses that Jesus is the "created" rather than "begotten" Word of the Father.[26] This unsubstantiated substitution of words is meant to deny the pre-existence of Jesus by showing him to be a creature of God, rather than God himself.

Rejection of a Personal Holy Spirit. It follows from Wierwille's unitarian monotheism that he would reject the Holy Spirit as the third person of the Godhead just as he rejects the deity of Jesus Christ. He holds that "holy spirit" is a spiritual ability or power, lacking personality: "God is Holy and God is Spirit. The gift that He gives is holy spirit."[27] "Many people confuse the Giver, Holy Spirit, with the gift, holy spirit.... God, who is the Holy Spirit, can only give that which He is. Therefore, the gift of God is of necessity holy, *hagion,* and spirit, *pneuma.*"[28] "*Pneuma hagion* as used in the New Testament regarding that which was received into manifestation on the Day of Pentecost always referred to what the Giver, Holy Spirit, God, gave.... Therefore the gift from the Giver is of necessity holy and spirit. The gift is holy spirit, *pneuma hagion,* which is an inherent spiritual ability, *dunamis,* power from on high."[29]

One thing is clear from Wierwille's explanation—the Holy Spirit is *not* a person, but an impersonal power or ability. But the Bible reveals that *pneuma hagion* is something greater than an impersonal power or enablement (though not less than that). Scripture shows *pneuma hagion* to be a distinct person with a mind, a will, emotions and power of his own. Jesus himself reveals the personality of the Holy Spirit in some of his parting words to his disciples: "But the Counselor, the Holy Spirit, whom the Father will send in my name, he will teach you all things, and bring to your remembrance all that I have said to you.... But when the Counselor comes, whom I shall send to you from the Father, even the Spirit of truth, who proceeds from the Father, he will bear witness to me.... When the Spirit of truth comes, he will guide you into all the truth; for he will not speak on his own authority, but whatever he hears he will speak, and he will declare to you the things that are to come" (Jn 14:26; 15:26; 16:13).

So we see that the Holy Spirit can hear, speak, teach, comfort, remind, convict, guide, reveal future things (and even be grieved;

184

see Eph 4:30). Wierwille is right to think that *pneuma hagion* is distinct from the Father; he is wrong to teach that this means that the Holy Spirit is an impersonal gift, power or ability. With the Father and the Son, the Holy Spirit is a member of the three-personed Godhead.

Wierwille is also correct in stating that there is no single Bible passage which clearly defines the doctrine of the Trinity. But he either ignores or discards those passages which speak of the unity and distinctness of the three persons. Considering only Wierwille's preferred Scriptures, the Epistles, we find many such passages. To the Corinthians Paul says, "Now there are varieties of gifts, but the same Spirit; and there are varieties of service, but the same Lord; and there are varieties of working, but it is the same God who inspires them all" (1 Cor 12:4-6). At the close of another letter to the Corinthians Paul blesses them in this way: "The grace of the Lord Jesus Christ and the love of God and the fellowship of the Holy Spirit be with you all" (2 Cor 13:14).

The unity of God and his triune nature are affirmed by Paul in one statement to the church at Ephesus: "There is one body and one Spirit, just as you were called to the one hope that belongs to your call, one Lord, one faith, one baptism, one God and Father of us all" (Eph 4:4-6).

Misunderstanding of Redemption. A doctrine closely linked with the divine-human nature of Jesus, and crucial to the Christian faith, is his role as Savior or Redeemer. Wierwille makes his position plain: "Separating the Father from the Son does not at all discredit the Son.... Rather, trinitarian dogma... degrades God from his elevated, unparalleled position; besides, it leaves man unredeemed."[30] And elsewhere he says, "If Jesus Christ is God and not the Son of God, we have not yet been redeemed."[31]

In the latter statement Wierwille is asserting that it requires a human to die on behalf of other humans. That is true; but it requires a perfect, divine sacrifice to be *adequate* (see Heb 10). And that is just the point—Jesus Christ is the God-man.

The Jewish people had always sought to have a redeemed relationship with God, to exist with God in the perfect relationship which God had sought to inaugurate through the covenants with Noah, Abraham and Moses. While the Jews knew that they had erred from God's ways, they continually sought to make an offering to bring themselves into a righteous relationship. Even in Jesus' day people brought lambs or doves to the temple for sacrifice in order to effect a "propitiation" or perfect offering for sin.

These sacrifices, being but imperfect shadows of the true sacrifice of Jesus Christ, could "never take away sins" (Heb 10:11). But God has prepared a better sacrifice for our redemption—the life of his Son: "Since all have sinned and fall short of the glory of God, they are justified by his grace as a gift, through the redemption which is in Christ Jesus, whom God put forward as an expiation [propitiation] by his blood, to be received by faith" (Rom 3:23-25; see also 1 Jn 2:2; 4:10).

The essential tie between his redemptive work and his divinity was stressed by Jesus himself: "He said to them [the Jews], 'You are from below, I am from above; you are of this world, I am not of this world. I told you that you would die in your sins, for you will die in your sins unless you believe that I am he' " (Jn 8:23-24). Of this last expression, "I am he," Leon Morris says, "We should probably understand it along the lines of the similar expression in LXX [the Greek translation of the Old Testament], which is the style of deity (cf. Is 43:10). . . . Unless we believe that He is more than man we can never trust Him with that faith that is saving faith."[32] Because Jesus was divine, God the Son as well as the Son of God, he was able to redeem humanity. Wierwille's interpretations of Scripture totally deny this essential element of Christian doctrine.

Necessity of Tongues. The Way's teaching on tongues is another prominent and serious problem. The fact that The Way emphasizes the spiritual gifts puts it, in that respect, in company with many orthodox Christians. The problem stems from Wierwille's teaching that speaking in tongues is the acceptable sign of true worship: "To worship by the spirit we must operate a manifestation of the holy spirit. The manifestation of the spirit which produces true worship is speaking in tongues."[33]

Wierwille teaches further that speaking in tongues is the necessary indication that a person has been "born again." His defense is based on his interpretation of the book of Acts: "Every place in the Book of Acts where the holy spirit was received and the initial external manifestation is mentioned, it is always speaking in tongues."[34] Consequently, in the PFAL classes Wierwille teaches his method for speaking in tongues: "I am ministering the holy spirit to you, teaching you exactly what to do.... Sit quietly and do exactly as I instruct.... Open your mouth wide and breathe in.... You are now going to manifest the spirit's presence.... Move your lips, your throat, your tongue. Speak forth.... The external manifestation is your proof in the sense world that you have Christ within."[35]

Though Wierwille supposedly gets his authority for teaching that every Christian must speak in tongues from Acts, Luke's account, in fact, does not indicate that tongues always accompanied conversion and the receiving of the Holy Spirit (see the account of the Samaritan converts in Acts 8:14-17). And though the account of Paul's conversion in Acts 9 says that Paul received the Holy Spirit and was baptized by Ananias, it says nothing about speaking in tongues (though we know from 1 Corinthians 14:18 that Paul later did speak in tongues).

Furthermore, no Scripture suggests that speaking in tongues produces or is necessary for true worship. On the contrary, while discussing the church as the body of Christ (1 Cor 12:7-10), Paul makes it very clear that just as each member of the body contributes something different to its functioning, so to each member of Christ's body "is given the manifestation of the Spirit for the common good. To one is given ... wisdom, and to another ... knowledge ... to another ... to another" and so on. "All these," he concludes, "are inspired by one and the same Spirit, who apportions to each one individually as he wills" (12:11). In other words, the Spirit decides who manifests which gift. Finally, in the same chapter Paul asks, "Are all apostles? Are all prophets? Are all teachers? Do all work miracles? Do all possess gifts of healing? Do all speak with tongues?" (12:29-30). The implied answer is no, for to answer otherwise is to nullify the notion of the church as the *body* of Christ.[36]

Speaking in tongues, like the other gifts, is given to some and not to others, according to the will of the Holy Spirit. It is not a necessary condition or sign of true worship or conversion.

If These Things Are So

What are we to think of Wierwille's teaching? What are its fruits? Certainly The Way has helped some to overcome drug addiction. But some former Way followers join with some parents in alleging that The Way has caused emotional harm to some adherents and that children have been cut off from their parents by The Way's teaching and influence. And without doubt Wierwille's denial of the personality of the Holy Spirit and the deity of Christ is heretical. Wierwille says that "the Word means what it says, and it says what it means." But in spite of this, he repeatedly ignores explicit teaching in the very Scriptures he claims are his foundation. Clearly the Word means and says what The Way wants it to say.

Most Way believers are totally sincere and motivated by a genuine spiritual yearning. The apostle Paul understood this yearning and the answer God provides: "He saved us, not because of deeds done by us in righteousness, but in virtue of his own mercy, by the washing of regeneration and renewal in the Holy Spirit" (Tit 3:5). We can never buy God's grace, not by outright purchase (as Simon the magician attempted in Acts 8) nor by payments for "Power for Abundant Living" courses offered by The Way. Though The Way purports to satisfy the spiritual hunger of these people, the teachings of Victor Paul Wierwille are so different from biblical truth at crucial points as to be without spiritual nourishment. Jesus warned, "Beware of false prophets, who come to you in sheep's clothing but inwardly are ravenous wolves. You will know them by their fruits" (Mt 7:15-16).

If you are a follower of The Way, you may be disturbed about some of the information presented here about a movement which may have provided you with the first really loving fellowship you have ever experienced. I mean to speak truthfully, not to malign anyone or disparage your experience.

Nevertheless, it is true that a careful reading of Scripture will reveal Wierwille's inconsistencies. We must meet people on their chosen ground, and Wierwille has chosen the Bible. Often his interpretations are demonstrably contrary to the clear teachings of Scripture. For example, in one study Wierwille states, "The records of baptism in Acts, the book which records the events of Pentecost and immediately thereafter, do not mention water at all; thus to say there is water involved in baptism can only be private interpretation."[37] Now, take your Bible and compare what the Scripture itself says in Acts 8:36-38: "And as they went along the road they came to some water, and the eunuch said, 'See, here is water! What is to prevent my being baptized?' And he commanded the chariot to stop, and they both went down into the water, Philip and the eunuch, and he baptized him." And on another occasion Peter said, "Can any one forbid water for baptizing these people who have received the Holy Spirit just as we have? And he commanded them to be baptized" (Acts 10:47-48).

Examples such as this one or the discussion earlier in this chapter concerning the deity of Jesus Christ and the Holy Spirit raise serious questions (at the very least) about the accuracy of Wierwille's teaching.

Are you willing to do a careful study of John 1 and Colossians 1 *on your own*, apart from the interpretations of The Way? The people of the city of Beroea were called "noble" because they "received the word with all eagerness, *examining the scriptures daily to see if these things were so*" (Acts 17:10-11). If these early Christians were called noble for checking the teachings of the apostle Paul to see if they agreed with Scripture, how much more appropriate is it for all of us today to do the same with teachers we encounter?

Jesus Christ, the Incarnation of God, is the only Lord and Savior.

Faith is the key to our salvation, but that faith must include an acceptance and acknowledgment of his identity, of who he *is*, as well as what he has done for us on the cross. He is the one who said, "I am the way, and the truth, and the life; no one comes to the Father, but by me" (Jn 14:6).

12
Evaluating Cults and New Religions
LaVonne Neff

I believe in God, the Father almighty,
creator of heaven and earth.
I believe in Jesus Christ, his only Son, our Lord.
He was conceived by the power of the Holy Spirit
and born of the Virgin Mary.
He suffered under Pontius Pilate,
was crucified, died, and was buried.
He descended to the dead.
On the third day he rose again.
He ascended into heaven,
and is seated at the right hand of the Father.
He will come again to judge the living and the dead.
I believe in the Holy Spirit,
the holy catholic Church,
the communion of saints,
the forgiveness of sins,
the resurrection of the body,
and the life everlasting. Amen.
The Apostles' Creed

CHAPTER ONE, "WHAT IS A CULT?" showed how difficult it can be to define the word *cult*. There is a world of difference between the movement founded by Bhagwan Shree Rajneesh, say, and the Latter-day Saints, yet both have been called cults. At different times and in different places, Lutherans and Mennonites and Methodists have also been called cults. For that matter, so has the entire Christian church.

A cult is a small group that considers a larger group to be dead wrong. The first Christians criticized both pagan Rome and traditional Judaism. Lutherans broke with the Renaissance papacy. Mennonites stood apart from all institutionalized sixteenth-century churches. And Methodists combated the moral laziness they saw in eighteenth-century Anglicanism.

Some cults have, in the long run, built up the Christian church by giving it more zeal, fresh insights, stronger commitment. Others have separated from the Christian church either to create rival institutions or to quietly fade away. To the church, however, any cult is a potential threat because it is an accusation. It is saying that the church is inadequate or wrong.

Obviously the church, made up of human beings, is often inadequate and sometimes wrong. Merely pointing out the church's faults does not make a group evil or dangerous. The biblical prophets, after all, did not mince words. So how can Christians evaluate cults, new religions and other groups that share cultic characteristics?

First, it is important to compare a group's teachings with basic Christian doctrine. In spite of differences between Baptists and Presbyterians, Methodists and Catholics, Christians of all denominations still share certain basic beliefs. Strip these away and what you have left is not Christianity.

Second, it is equally important to look at how the group affects people's lives. We humans are not disembodied intellects. We have emotional and physical needs. We live in a web of relationships that include family, coworkers, friends and neighbors. Good religion must be doctrinally sound, and it must also have positive effects on people's everyday lives.

New Religions and Christian Teaching
In this book we have looked at ten cults or new religions in the light of biblical Christian teachings. Since each group abandons orthodoxy at a different point, each chapter has looked at a different part of the Christian faith. But it is important, in evaluating

cults and new religions, to keep in mind the overall picture of Christianity found in all Christian churches. (See the reading list on page 214 for suggestions on further reading in basic Christianity.)

The earliest Christians asked baptismal candidates three questions: Do you believe in God? Do you believe in his Son, Jesus Christ? Do you believe in the Holy Spirit? Candidates' answers to these questions soon developed into the Apostles' Creed, presented in a modern translation at the beginning of this chapter. This creed is used in Roman Catholic and many Protestant churches today, and the churches that do not use creeds still agree with its statements. It is therefore a helpful reminder of basic Christian teachings.

I believe in God, the Father almighty, creator of heaven and earth. The god of Eastern religions and their cultic derivatives (Bhagwan Shree Rajneesh, Eckankar, Hare Krishna, Transcendental Meditation and many others) is the animating force of creation but is not the Creator. Their god does not distinguish between good and evil because it (not he or she) is equally present in all that exists. It is not personal; in fact, Eastern religious movements often see individual personality as something to overcome. The ultimate goal of Eastern religion is to merge one's personality with the One, the god of no personality who is one with all things.

By contrast, Christians, Jews and Muslims understand God as the powerful Creator of everything that exists. Existing eternally, he is greater than his creation, yet he makes himself known through the things he has created. He is continuously involved in maintaining and directing his universe. To use philosophical terms, God is both transcendent (above his creation) and immanent (within his creation).

This God is not merely a force or a power. He is a person. He relates to other persons, and he wants them to relate to him. He is completely loving and totally good in all that he does. In fact, human ideas of love and goodness come from God.

I believe in Jesus Christ, his only Son, our Lord. Half the groups discussed in this book agree that God is both transcendent and immanent, both personal and loving. They disagree, however, about Jesus.

Cults and new religions almost always recognize Jesus as a great teacher. Eastern-inspired groups may describe him as an avatar, an incarnation of the One. Western groups are more likely to see him as a wise man or even as the most important of God's created beings. But no group described in this book understands Jesus to be fully human and fully divine in a unique, unrepeatable sense.

Christians believe that Jesus is both divine and human. He is not God in temporary human clothing. He is not a divinely enlightened man. He is fully God and fully man—a fact which Christians accept, even if we cannot completely explain it. Furthermore, Jesus' nature is unique. He is not one of a succession of God-men. He is the only person in all history to be both divine and human.

Christians also believe that Jesus is our Savior. God is perfectly good, and anything bad is foreign to his nature. Although he has permitted evil to invade his good universe, someday he will destroy everything bad. This would be welcome news except for one fact—we humans are not so good ourselves. All of us have sins, flaws, problems; whatever we call our faults, they have turned the world into a dangerous place. Does this mean that we will be destroyed when God cleans up the universe?

We don't have to be. Part of God's goodness is his love for us. God sent Jesus to do what we couldn't do by ourselves. We cannot live perfectly good lives, but Jesus did. We by rights should die and be separated from God, but Jesus died the death of separation in our place. We should have no hope for the future, but Jesus rose from the dead and proclaimed that we too can be raised to eternal life with God.

What can we do to receive eternal life? The cults and new religions all prescribe human acts to assure eternal bliss or at least absence of pain. The Christian answer stands in sharp contrast: We must believe that Jesus offers life to us as a gift from God. We cannot earn a place in heaven by good actions, sacrifices, rituals or prayers. We do not need to earn a place because one is already reserved for us by God, who wants only our love in return. Our Scriptures and our great thinkers insist that "the free gift of God is eternal life in Christ Jesus our Lord" (Rom 6:23).

I believe in the Holy Spirit. Eastern cults, though they often believe in spirits, have nothing resembling the Holy Spirit. Western cults, if they believe in the Holy Spirit at all, often depersonalize him or severely limit his activity. And even some Christian groups—groups that completely agree with orthodox teachings about God and Jesus—tend to limit the work of the Holy Spirit, believing he is active in a special way in their own group but not in the church as a whole.

The Christian church, however, teaches that God works in the whole world in the person of his Holy Spirit. The Holy Spirit works with *all people,* pointing out sin and turning them to Jesus. He works with *the Christian church* in particular, giving people gifts that will strengthen it (the Bible is one of the Spirit's most important gifts to the church). He works with *individuals* as well, assuring them of their salvation and making them resemble Jesus, their Lord. In all that he does, the Holy Spirit draws attention not to individual Christians nor to himself but to Jesus.

All the groups discussed in this book believe the Christian church is wrong. Most also believe that truth is their own exclusive property. None believes that God's Holy Spirit is present and active in a special way in the Christian church. But even within the Christian communion, some groups are beginning to question the Spirit's presence in Christianity as a whole. Such groups charge that the church is spiritually lazy, doctrinally impure, morally corrupt. The Spirit will not tolerate such wickedness. Come to our group, they say: our doctrine is pure, our discipline rigorous. Here and only here you will be blessed.

Such groups are not unchristian. They do not deny the infinite-personal God after the manner of Eastern cults. They do not deny the Christian view of the nature and work of Christ after the manner of Western cults. Their criticisms of the church may be well

195

founded. Are such groups prophetic movements raised up by God to purify his church, or are they the beginnings of cults that will only divide it?

Answering this question requires a great deal of discernment. Nobody welcomes prophets, and it is easy to dismiss all criticism as divisive, cultic and sub-Christian. On the other hand, even divinely inspired prophetic movements risk degenerating into splinter movements if they lose sight of their original purpose of building up the body of Christ. Do fringe Christian groups reject the work of the Holy Spirit in the whole Christian church, or do they see themselves working with him on behalf of the church? How does membership in this group affect people's lives? To answer this question, we must turn from theology to practice.

Looking at Results

Some cult watchers make a serious mistake: they assume that if they can prove a group's teachings false or absurd, they can then persuade people to leave the group. Such an approach will work with some people, but most have needs that far outweigh their perceived need for truth. People do not usually base their attraction to the Mormon Church, for example, on a conviction that Joseph Smith was a hieroglyphics expert. Instead, they are attracted by the Mormon way of life with its emphasis on traditional American values.

In evaluating cults and new religions, it is important to consider the effects such groups have on individuals who join them. Good results will not sanctify bad doctrine, but bad results can serve as warning lights, even where teaching appears sound. In some cases, looking at the group's effect on its members' lives may be the only way to distinguish between a cult and a prophetic Christian movement. What happens to members' personalities, relationships, job commitments, community involvement? Is the group's overall effect on those who come in contact with it—members and nonmembers—positive or negative? Is it an agency of healing, restoration and reconciliation? Consider the following questions:

1. Does a member's personality generally become stronger, happier, more confident as a result of contact with the group?

2. Do members of the group seek to deepen and strengthen their family commitments?

3. Does the group encourage independent thinking and the development of discernment skills?

4. Does the group allow for individual differences of belief and behavior, particularly in areas of less-than-central importance?

5. Does the group encourage high moral standards both among members and between members and nonmembers?

6. Does the group's leadership invite dialog, advice and evaluation from outside its own immediate circle?

7. Does the group allow for development in theological beliefs?

8. Are group members encouraged to ask the hard questions without threat of reprisal of any kind?

9. Do group members appreciate truth wherever it is found, even if it is outside their group?

10. Is the group honest in dealing with nonmembers, especially as it tries to win them to the group?

11. Does the group foster relationships and linkages with the larger society—connections that are more than self-serving?

How Cults Can Help the Church

This book has focused on the errors of cults and new religious movements. The authors have analyzed both teaching and practice to show that cults are a poor substitute for the Christian church. Yet cults can help the church if the church is willing to be helped.

Even in their excesses, many cults have features that Christians should sit up and notice. Eckists hunger for contact with spiritual reality. Baha'is long for world peace. Mormons work to build strong families. Jehovah's Witnesses are eager to tell others about their faith. Devotees of Transcendental Meditation practice spiritual discipline.

Why have these people found answers to their needs in cults and new religions rather than in the Christian church? Can the church listen to what cult members are saying and, in turn, show them how Jesus meets their needs? Can the church—your congregation and mine—create an environment that will welcome searchers and help them grow up into Christ?

Cults and new religions will not evaporate in the heat of Christian argument. They may, however, lose their reason to exist where the Christian church is alive and well. If the persistent presence of cults causes Christians to take a hard look at our own faith and practice, they will indeed be doing us a great service.

Notes

Chapter 1: What Is a Cult?

[1]*SCP Journal*, September 1979, p. 50.

[2]Julia Cass, "A Bad Karma on Main Line," *Philadelphia Inquirer*, 28 September 1980.

[3]Letter to the Editor, *Philadelphia Inquirer*, 8 December 1980.

[4]Thomas Robbins, "Religious Movements, the State, and the Law: Reconceptualizing 'The Cult Problem,' " *New York University Review of Law and Social Change* 9, no. 1 (1980-81): 33.

[5]Brooks Alexander, "What Is a Cult?" *SCP Newsletter*, January/February 1979.

[6]James W. Sire, *Scripture Twisting* (Downers Grove, Ill.: InterVarsity Press, 1980), p. 20.

[7]John Lofland, *Doomsday Cult* (Englewood Cliffs, N.J.: Prentice-Hall, 1966), p. 1.

[8]Sire, *Scripture Twisting*, p. 20.

[9]James Bjornstad, *Counterfeits at Your Door* (Glendale, Calif.: Regal Books, 1979), p. 152.

[10]Sun Myung Moon, "Holy Wine Ceremony," trans. Bo Hi Pak, *The Blessing Quarterly* 1 (Spring 1977): 3.

[11]Ibid., p. 19.

[12]Bryan Wilson, *Religion in Sociological Perspective* (New York: Oxford University Press, 1982), p. 12.

[13]Ronald Enroth, "Cult/Countercult," *Eternity*, November 1977, p. 35.

[14]Personal letter dated 29 April 1982.

[15]Robert S. Ellwood, *Alternative Altars* (Chicago: University of Chicago Press, 1979), p. 19.

[16]Moon, "Holy Wine Ceremony," p. 5.

[17]*A Way of Life: Code of Conduct for Students of Summit University* (Malibu, Calif.: Summit University Press, 1978), p. 13.

[18]Bhagwan Shree Rajneesh, "Laugh Your Way to God," *Rajneesh Foundation Newsletter*, 1 December 1981, p. 3.

[19]John Robert Stevens, *Counsel for Counselors* (North Hollywood, Calif.: Living Word Publications, 1971), pp. 34-35.

[20]Mard Naman, "The Pure Ones," *New West*, 1 December 1980, p. 94.

[21]*New York Times*, 5 November 1981.

[22]Ed Mitchell et al., *The Truth* (Hesperia, Calif.: The Truth Station, 1980), p. 139.

[23]Brooks Alexander, "The Rise of Cosmic Humanism," *SCP Journal* 5 (Winter 1981-82): 3-4.

[24]Wilson, *Religion in Sociological Perspective*, p. 91.

[25]Ibid., pp. 111-13.

[26]Ronald Enroth, *The Lure of the Cults* (Downers Grove, Ill.: InterVarsity Press, 1983).

[27]Thomas Robbins and Dick Anthony, "The Limits of 'Coercive Persuasion' as an Explanation for Conversion to Authoritarian Sects," *Political Psychology* 2 (Summer 1980): 23.

[28]Mark Albrecht and Brooks Alexander, "Jonestown Once More," *SCP Newsletter*, January/February 1979.

Chapter 2: The Baha'i Faith

[1]For a pronunciation guide to difficult foreign words, see p. 41.

[2]Edward G. Browne, "Bab, Babis," *Encyclopaedia of Religion and Ethics*, 1928 ed., p. 301.

[3]Ibid. See also Browne, *A Year amongst the Persians*, 3rd ed. (London: A. & C. Black, Ltd., 1950; reprint 1959), pp. 226-27.

[4]Ibid., *Encyclopaedia*, p. 302.

[5]Shoghi Effendi, *The World Order of Baha'u'llah* (Wilmette, Ill: Baha'i Publishing Trust, 1955), p. 133.

[6]Abdu'l-Baha, *Will and Testament of Abdu'l-Baha* (Wilmette: Baha'i Publishing Trust, 1971), p. 26.

[7]Shoghi Effendi, *God Passes By* (Wilmette: Baha'i Publishing Trust, 1970), p. 214. See also Abdu'l-Baha, *Will*, pp. 11-12, and "In the Hands of the Hands," *Time*, 9 December 1957, p. 87.

[8]Shoghi Effendi, *World Order of Baha'u'llah*, p. 115.

[9]Shoghi Effendi, *God Passes By*, pp. 93-96.

[10]Baha'u'llah, *Gleanings from the Writings of Baha'u'llah*, rev. ed. (Wilmette: Baha'i Publishing Trust, 1952), pp. 319-20. Baha'u'llah, quoted in Shoghi Effendi, *God Passes By*, p. 99. Baha'u'llah, *Gleanings*, p. 245. Baha'u'llah, quoted in Shoghi Effendi, *World Order of Baha'u'llah*, pp. 103-4.

[11]Baha'u'llah, *The Seven Valleys and the Four Valleys* (Wilmette: Baha'i Publishing Trust, 1952), pp. 39-40.

[12]Universal House of Justice, *A Synopsis and Codification of the Kitab-i-Aqdas* (Welwyn Garden City, England: Broadwater Press, Ltd., 1973), pp. 35-65; also Baha'u'llah, *Al-Kitab, Al-Aqdas*, trans. Earl E. Elder and

William McE. Miller (London: The Royal Asiatic Society, 1961), reprint as Appendix I in Miller, *The Baha'i Faith: Its History and Teachings* (S. Pasadena, Calif.: William Carey Library, 1974).

[13]Shoghi Effendi, *World Order of Baha'u'llah*, pp. 7, 19, 36-48.

[14]Ibid., pp. 40-41.

[15]Gerald B. Parks, "The Necessity of a Utopia," *World Order* journal (Fall 1974).

[16]Shoghi Effendi, *World Order of Baha'u'llah*, p. 5.

[17]Abdu'l-Baha, quoted in Shoghi Effendi, *World Order of Baha'u'llah*, p. 39. See also John Esslemont, *Baha'u'llah and the New Era*, 3rd rev. ed. (Wilmette: Baha'i Publishing Trust, 1970), p. 251.

[18]Abdu'l-Baha, *Some Answered Questions* (Wilmette: Baha'i Publishing Trust, 1930), p. 97. See John 10:38; 17:21.

[19]Shoghi Effendi, *God Passes By*, pp. 188, 348.

[20]Abdu'l-Baha, *Some Answered Questions*, pp. 119-21.

[21]Ibid., p. 195.

[22]Baha'u'llah, *Kitabi-Iqan* (Wilmette: Baha'i Publishing Trust, 1931), p. 154.

[23]Esslemont, *Baha'u'llah and the New Era*, 1923 ed., p. 212. Later editions, published after Esslemont's death, change the date to 1963 and impute a different and indefinite meaning to the year.

[24]Quoted in Shoghi Effendi, *God Passes By*, p. 92. Browne says, "The theory now advanced by the Baha'is that the Bab considered himself as a mere herald or forerunner of the Dispensation which Baha'u'llah was shortly to establish, and was to him what John the Baptist was to Jesus Christ, is . . . devoid of historic foundation. In his own eyes, as in the eyes of his followers, [the Bab] inaugurated a new Prophetic Cycle, and brought a new Revelation" (quoted by Miller, *The Baha'i Faith*, pp. 53-54).

[25]Abdu'l-Baha, *Some Answered Questions*, p. 125.

[26]Baha'u'llah, *Gleanings from the Writings of Baha'u'llah*, pp. 330-31.

[27]Universal House of Justice, *Synopsis*, note #17, p. 59. See *Al-Kitab Al-Aqdas* in Miller, *The Baha'i Faith*, p. 40.

[28]Browne, *A Year amongst the Persians*, pp. 343-44. An official synopsis and codification of the laws of the *Aqdas* is available to Baha'is. See note 12. See Miller, *The Baha'i Faith*, pp. 323-26.

[29]Quoted in Esslemont, *Baha'u'llah and the New Era*, 1970 ed., p. 181.

[30]Shoghi Effendi, *World Order of Baha'u'llah*, pp. 202, 157.

[31]Quoted in Shoghi Effendi, *Advent of Divine Justice* (Wilmette: Baha'i Publishing Trust, 1939), p. 24.

[32]For evidences that Christ's resurrection was of the body, see Josh Mc-

Dowell, *Evidence That Demands a Verdict* (San Bernardino, Calif.: Campus Crusade for Christ, 1972), chapter 10; also Frank Morison, *Who Moved the Stone?* (Downers Grove, Ill.: InterVarsity Press, 1958).
[33]See also 2 Corinthians 5:15.

Chapter 3: Bhagwan Shree Rajneesh
[1]Ma Ananda Sarita, ed., *Bhagwan Shree Rajneesh Diary–1979* (Bombay: Rajneesh Foundation, 1978), p. 4.
[2]Ibid., p. 5.
[3]Ibid., p. 11.
[4]Quoted in *Orange Juice*, newsletter of the Rajneesh Meditation Center, San Francisco, Calif., September 1981.
[5]Sarita, *Rajneesh Diary*, pp. 33-34.
[6]Ibid., p. 35.
[7]*Orange Juice* newsletter, September 1981.
[8]This statement was made in the hearing of the author.
[9]Bhagwan Shree Rajneesh, *I Am the Gate* (New York: Harper & Row, 1977), pp. 5, 82.
[10]Ibid., p. 73.
[11]*Sannyas* magazine (Bombay), January 1980.
[12]Sarita, *Rajneesh Diary*, p. 25.
[13]Rajneesh, *I Am the Gate*, p. 73.
[14]Ibid., p. 132.
[15]This statement is typical of ones the author has heard many times.
[16]Rajneesh, *I Am the Gate*, p. 65.
[17]Ibid., pp. 1, 7.
[18]*The Mind of Acharya Rajneesh* (Bombay: Jaico Publishing House, 1974), pp. 224, 252, 256.
[19]Rajneesh, *I Am the Gate*, p. 12.
[20]Ibid., p. 5.
[21]*Sannyas*, April 1978, p. 18.
[22]Bhagwan Shree Rajneesh, *Roots and Wings: Talks on Zen* (London: Routledge and Kegan Paul, 1979), p. 467. Cf. Jn 4:14; 7:37.
[23]John R. W. Stott, *The Authority of the Bible* (Downers Grove, Ill.: InterVarsity Press, 1974), p. 7.
[24]Quoted in M. M. Malatesta, "In Search of the Cosmic Orgasm," *The Soho News* (New York), 20 October 1981, p. 15.

Chapter 4: Eckankar
[1]Paul Twitchell, *The Precepts of Eckankar* (Eckankar ASOST, n.d.), no. 3, p. 4.

[2]Paul Twitchell, *Illuminated Way Letters 1966-1971* (San Diego: Illuminated Way Press, 1975), pp. 230, 232-33.

[3]Darwin Gross, "Security with Eck," *Eck World News*, October 1978, pp. 10-11.

[4]Paul Twitchell, *The Shariyat-Ki-Sugmad* (San Diego: Illuminated Way Press, 1970-71), 1:130.

[5]Paul Twitchell, *Eckankar: The Secret Way* (Eckankar ASOST, 1967), no. 7, p. 1.

[6]Twitchell, *Shariyat*, 1:72, 83.

[7]Paul Twitchell, *The Eck Satsang Discourses*, 2nd ser. (Eckankar ASOST, 1970-71), no. 8, p. 6.

[8]Paul Twitchell, *Soul Travel: The Illuminated Way* (Eckankar ASOST, 1967), no. 9, p. 3.

[9]Twitchell, *Shariyat*, 1:149.

[10]Paul Twitchell, *The Tiger's Fang* (Eckankar ASOST, 1967), pp. iv, 43, 123.

[11]Twitchell, *Eckankar*, no. 7, p. 5.

[12]Twitchell, *Tiger's Fang*, p. 44.

[13]Paul Twitchell, *The Eck Master Discourses*, 1st ser. (Eckankar ASOST, 1970), no. 1, p. 1.

[14]Twitchell, *Soul Travel*, no. 9, p. 3.

[15]Twitchell, *Shariyat*, 1:93.

[16]Twitchell, *Tiger's Fang*, p. 91.

[17]Twitchell, *Eckankar*, no. 2, p. 1.

[18]Twitchell, *Soul Travel*, no. 1, p. 5.

[19]Bernadine Burlin, "The Blue Star of Eck: A Reality in the Spiritual Quest," *Eck Mata Journal* 2 (1977-78):11.

[20]Paul Twitchell, *The Spiritual Notebook* (San Diego: Illuminated Way Press, 1971), p. 75.

[21]Twitchell, *Satsang Discourses*, 1st ser., no. 3, p. 2.

[22]Ibid., 1st ser., no. 4, p. 1.

[23]Twitchell, *Precepts of Eckankar*, no. 2, p. 3.

[24]Twitchell, *Satsang Discourses*, 2d ser., no. 6, p. 1.

[25]Ibid., 2d ser., no. 3, p. 5.

[26]Darwin Gross, "The Golden Precepts of Eckankar," *Eck Mata Journal* 2 (1977-78):27.

[27]Twitchell, *Satsang Discourses*, 1st ser., no. 1, pp. 1, 6; 1st ser., no. 6, p. 4.

[28]Twitchell, *Precepts of Eckankar*, no. 8, p. 5.

[29]Twitchell, *Satsang Discourses*, 3d ser., no. 3, p. 1; 2d ser., no. 6, p. 1.

[30]Ibid., 3d ser., no. 3, pp. 3-4.

[31]Dhana Markley, Eckankar public relations spokeswoman, in a letter to *The Movement* newspaper (published in Los Angeles by the Movement

of Spiritual Inner Awareness) 3, no. 12 (n.d.):3.

[32]Paul Twitchell, Letters to a Chela, 1st ser. (Eckankar ASOST, 1972), no. 3, p. 1.

Chapter 5: est

[1]Adelaide Bry, est: 60 Hours That Transform Your Life (New York: Harper & Row, 1976), p. 9.

[2]Ibid., p. 78.

[3]Ibid., pp. 165-66.

[4]John Ruskin Clark, "Secular Salvation: Life Changes through 'est,' " Christian Century, 10 November 1976, p. 984.

[5]Bry, est: 60 Hours, pp. 13, 52.

[6]"Delegation of Werner Erhard and Associates to the All-Union Institute for Systems Studies," a paper of Werner Erhard and Associates presented in Moscow, 1981, p. 6; "Success Builds a Network," Graduate Review, July-August 1981, pp. 3-5.

[7]"The Trainer Body—Getting on with It," Graduate Review (magazine of the est organization currently titled The Review), August 1978, p. 10.

[8]Jerry Rubin, "The est Things in Life Aren't Free," Crawdaddy, February 1976, p. 41.

[9]The others included Mike Maurer, who eventually joined Scientology, and Peter Monk, who was already a member. William Warren Bartley III, Werner Erhard: The Transformation of a Man, the Founding of est (New York: Clarkson N. Potter, 1978), pp. 146-48.

[10]R. C. Devon Heck and Jennifer L. Thompson, "est, Salvation or Swindle?" San Francisco, January 1976, p. 70; see Nathanial Lande, Mindstyles, Lifestyles (Los Angeles: Price/Stern/Sloan Publishers, 1976), especially the section on Mind Dynamics.

[11]Bartley, Werner Erhard, pp. 14, 37, 75-76, 81-82, 118-20, 145, 148, 158, 174.

[12]Michael Toms and Will Noffke, "Werner Erhard— An Interview with the Source of est: Part I," New Age Journal, no. 7, 15 September 1975, pp. 18-20.

[13]"Delegation of Werner Erhard and Associates," p. 2.

[14]Bry, est: 60 Hours, p. 45.

[15]John Leo, "est: 'There Is Nothing to Get,' " Time, 7 June 1976, p. 53.

[16]Mark Brewer, "We're Gonna Tear You Down and Put You Back Together," Psychology Today, August 1975, p. 40. Bry, est: 60 Hours, p. 52.

[17]Brewer, "We're Gonna Tear," p. 40.

[18]Bry, est: 60 Hours, p. 56.

[19]Brewer, "We're Gonna Tear," p. 40.

[20]William Greene, Est: Four Days to Make Your Life Work (New York: Simon and Schuster, 1976), pp. 68-69.

[21]Leo, "est: Nothing to Get," p. 54.

[22]Bry, *est: 60 Hours*, p. 59.

[23]Ibid., p. 60.

[24]Brewer, "We're Gonna Tear," pp. 88-89.

[25]Sheridan Fenwick, *Getting It: The Psychology of est* (New York: J. B. Lippincott, 1976), pp. 127-29.

[26]Leland E. Hinsie, M.D., and Robert F. Campbell, M.D., *Psychiatric Dictionary*, 4th ed. (New York: Oxford University Press, 1970), p. 466.

[27]Brewer, "We're Gonna Tear," p. 39.

[28]Richard P. Marsh, "The Case for est: 'I Am the Cause of My World,' " *Psychology Today*, August 1975, p. 38.

[29]Greene, *est: Four Days*, p. 171; cf. p. 132.

[30]Heck and Thompson, "est, Salvation or Swindle?" p. 71.

[31]Brewer, "We're Gonna Tear," p. 39.

[32]Luke Rhinehart, *The Book of est* (New York: Holt, Rinehart and Winston, 1976), pp. 259-60.

[33]Toms and Noffke, "Warner Erhard," p. 28; see also "Werner Erhard: 'All I Can Do Is Lie,' " *East-West Journal*, September 1974, est rpt., p. 2.

[34]Joel Kovel, *A Complete Guide to Therapy from Psychoanalysis to Behavior Modification* (New York: Pantheon Books, 1976), p. 172.

[35]L. L. Glass, M. A. Kirsch, F. N. Paris, "Psychiatric Disturbances Associated with Erhard Seminars Training (est) I: A Report of Cases," *American Journal of Psychiatry*, March 1977, pp. 245-47. M. A. Kirsch, L. L. Glass, "Psychiatric Disturbances Associated with Erhard Seminars Training (est) II: Additional Cases and Theoretical Considerations," *American Journal of Psychiatry*, November 1977, pp. 1254-58.

[36]Clark, "Secular Salvation," p. 981.

[37]Werner Erhard, "Taking the Mystery out of Mastery," *What's So* (magazine of the est organization), January 1975.

[38]Rhinehart, *Book of est*, back cover.

[39]Ibid., pp. 216-17.

[40]Donald Porter and Diane Taxson, *The est Experience* (New York: Award Books, 1976), p. 101.

[41]Ibid., p. 212.

[42]"Werner Erhard: 'All I Can Do Is Lie,' " p. 1.

[43]Bartley, *Werner Erhard*, pp. 118-20, 147-48; Toms and Noffke, "Werner Erhard," p. 20.

[44]"The est Foundation—The First Seven Years: 1973-1980," pp. 9-15 (supplement to *Graduate Review*, September-October 1981).

[45]Jerry Rubin, "I'm Scared, You're Scared," *New Age Journal*, no. 7, 15 September 1975, p. 44.

[46]"Werner Erhard: 'All I Can Do Is Lie,' " p. 5.
[47]Ibid., p. 2.
[48]Greene, Est: Four Days, p. 131.
[49]"What Is the Purpose of the est Training?" (an est brochure).
[50]Heck and Thompson, "est, Salvation or Swindle?" p. 23.
[51]Greene, Est: Four Days, pp. 29, 32.
[52]Peter Marin, Harper's, October 1975, p. 46.
[53]"Delegation of Werner Erhard and Associates," p. 10.
[54]Werner Erhard, "Life, Living, and Winning the Game," Graduate Review, July 1976, pp. 1-5; Toms and Noffke, "Werner Erhard," p. 3.
[55]Werner Erhard, "The Transformation of est," Graduate Review, November 1976, p. 10.

Chapter 6: Hare Krishna (ISKCON)
[1]Bhagavad-Gita, 6.27, 29, 47, trans. Swami Prabhupada; from the back cover of Swami Prabhupada, Krsna Consciousness: The Topmost Yoga System (Los Angeles: ISKCON Books, 1970).
[2]Cornelia Dimmitt & J. A. van Buitenen, Classical Hindu Mythology: A Reader in the Sanskrit Puranas (Philadelphia: Temple University Press, 1978), p. 59.
[3]Ibid., p. 62.
[4]Marvin Henry Harper, Gurus, Swamis, and Avatars (Philadelphia: Westminster Press, 1972), p. 230.
[5]Vishal Mangalwadi, The World of Gurus (New Delhi: Vikas Publishing House, 1977), p. 84.
[6]William Borders, "Hare Krishna leaders believe sect has won a broader base," Minneapolis Tribune, 22 January 1978.
[7]Faye Levine, The Strange World of the Hare Krishnas (New York: Fawcett Publications, 1974), p. 35.
[8]Mangalwadi, World of Gurus, p. 85.
[9]J. Stillson Judah, "The Hare Krishna Movement," in Religious Movements in Contemporary America, ed. Irving I. Zarestsky and Mark P. Leone (Princeton: Princeton University Press, 1974), p. 469.
[10]Levine, Strange World, p. 69.
[11]Ibid., p. 45.
[12]David Haddon, "Thou Shalt Not Think," HIS, December 1973, p. 10.
[13]Levine, Strange World, p. 60.
[14]John R. W. Stott, Christian Mission in the Modern World (Downers Grove, Ill.: InterVarsity Press, 1975), p. 72.
[15]Jacques Ellul, Prayer and Modern Man (New York: Seabury Press, 1973), p. 27.

Chapter 7: Jehovah's Witnesses

[1]William Miller, *Evidence from Scripture and History of the Second Coming of Christ about the Year 1843* (Boston: Joshua V. Himes, 1842). Miller arrived at his date by understanding the cleansing of the sanctuary after twenty-three hundred days (Dan 8:14) to refer to the cleansing of the world by Christ's return in twenty-three hundred years. The beginning point he derived from Daniel 9:25, which speaks of the directive to restore and build Jerusalem; Miller identified that event with Ezra's return in 457 B.C. The twenty-three hundred years from that date yield a date of 1843—or 1844, if one recognizes there is no zero in going from 1 B.C. to A.D. 1.

[2]N. H. Barbour and Charles T. Russell, *Three Worlds and the Harvest of This World* (Rochester, N.Y.: N. H. Barbour & C. T. Russell, 1877). The three worlds were regarded as the preflood "world that was," "the world that now is" and the future "world to come."

[3]*Watchtower*, 15 September 1910, p. 298.

[4]Charles T. Russell, *Thy Kingdom Come* (Brooklyn: International Bible Students Association, 1904), p. 342. The 1904 edition gives the corridor length as 3416 inches in length and concludes, "Thus the Pyramid witnesses that the close of 1874 was the chronological beginning of the time of trouble." The 1923 edition on the same page lengthens the corridor to 3457 inches and states, "Thus the Pyramid witnesses that the close of 1914 will be the beginning of the time of trouble."

[5]*Scottish Court of Sessions*, Douglas Walse v. James Latseim Clyde, Cs 258/2788 (November 1954); Pursuer's Proof, pp. 7, 61, 342-43.

[6]*Kingdom Ministry*, May 1974, p. 3.

[7]The translators requested that they remain anonymous, even after their death, but William Cetnar, who served at Watchtower headquarters at the time of the translation, named the five: N. H. Knorr, F. W. Franz, A. D. Schroeder, G. D. Gangas and M. Henschel (Edmond C. Gruss, *We Left Jehovah's Witnesses–A Non-Prophet Organization* [Phillipsburg, N.J.: Presbyterian & Reformed Publ. Co., 1974], p. 74).

[8]*Let God Be True* (Brooklyn: Watchtower Bible and Tract Society, 1952), pp. 101-2.

[9]Ibid., p. 108.

[10]Ibid., p. 32.

[11]Charles T. Russell, *The Time Is at Hand* (Brooklyn: WBTS, 1910), p. 129.

[12]*Let God Be True*, p. 138.

[13]*Make Sure of All Things* (Brooklyn: WBTS, 1950), p. 314.

[14]*The Truth Shall Make You Free* (Brooklyn: WBTS, 1943), p. 295.

[15]Joseph F. Rutherford, *Prophecy* (Brooklyn: WBTS, 1929), p. 65.

[16]*Watchtower,* 1 December 1981, p. 8.

[17]*Let God Be True,* p. 68.

[18]Ibid., pp. 92, 99.

[19]*Theocratic Aid to Kingdom Publishers* (Brooklyn: WBTS, 1945), pp. 249-50. *Watchtower,* 15 December 1972, p. 755.

[20]*Watchtower,* October-November 1881, p. 5.

[21]*Watchtower,* 15 July 1906, p. 215; 1 March 1896, p. 47; 15 June 1896, pp. 139-40; 1 September 1900, pp. 270-71.

[22]*Watchtower,* 1 December 1916, p. 367; 1 May 1922, pp. 131-32. *Watchtower* of December 15, 1922 (p. 396), even held that it was not only a fact but "a necessity of faith" to regard Russell as "that servant," and *Watchtower* of May 1, 1922 (p. 131), showed how doubting Russell leads to a complete overthrow of faith. Cf. J. F. Rutherford, *The Harp of God* (Brooklyn: WBTS, 1921), p. 239. The reference was completely deleted from the 1928 edition.

[23]*Watchtower,* 15 February 1927, p. 56; 1 August 1950, p. 230; 1 October 1967, p. 590; 15 January 1969, p. 51.

[24]*Watchtower* (15 December 1916, p. 391), referring to the importance of accepting Russell as "that servant," exclaimed, "To disregard the Message would mean to disregard the Lord."

[25]According to *Watchtower,* "The creature worshiper is unable to exercise the mind of Christ" or "to receive God's spirit" (1 May 1964, p. 270).

[26]*Watchtower,* 1 April 1972, p. 197. See also similar claims to be a prophet in *The Nations Shall Know That I Am Jehovah* (Brooklyn: WBTS, 1971), p. 70; *Watchtower,* 15 January 1969, pp. 40-41; 15 March 1972, p. 189.

[27]*Watchtower,* 1 March 1965, p. 151; *Aid to Bible Understanding* (Brooklyn: WBTS, 1971), p. 47.

[28]*Awake!* 8 October 1968, p. 23.

[29]Russell, *The Time Is at Hand,* p. 101.

[30]*Watchtower,* 1 September 1916, p. 265; Joseph F. Rutherford, *Millions Now Living Will Never Die* (Brooklyn: IBSA, 1920), pp. 89-90; *Watchtower,* 1 September 1922, p. 262; *Informant,* May 1940, p. 1; *Watchtower,* 15 September 1941, p. 288; *Awake!* 8 October 1968, p. 13. For documentary reprints concerning Watchtower prophetic failures, see Duane Magnani's *Eyes of Understanding.*

[31]In the "Scottish Court of Sessions" case cited above, Watchtower leaders admitted that they had, in fact, given false prophecies. Cf. Pursuer's Proof, pp. 103-5, 342-43.

Chapter 8: Latter-day Saints (Mormons)

[1]*Ensign* (periodical published by the corporation of the President of the

Church of Jesus Christ of Latter-day Saints), May 1981, p. 19.

[2]Ibid., p. 98.

[3]Joseph Smith, *History of the Church* (Salt Lake City: Deseret Book Company, 1978), 1:xxxix and lxviii.

[4]Ibid., p. xl.

[5]Ibid., p. xciv.

[6]Joseph Smith earlier had told conflicting stories of seeing only Christ or simply angels, and no revival occurred in his neighborhood in 1820 according to extant historical documents. The revival that led his family into the Presbyterian Church did not occur until the winter of 1824-25. For full documentation of this see Wesley P. Walters, *New Light on Mormon Origins from the Palmyra (N.Y.) Revival* (Salt Lake City: Modern Microfilm Company, 1967).

[7]David Whitmer, *An Address to All Believers in Christ* (1887; reprint ed., Concord, Calif.: Pacific Publishing Company, n.d.), p. 8.

[8]Smith, *History*, 1:40-42, 61.

[9]Ibid., pp. 82-83.

[10]Gordon Hinckley, *Truth Restored* (Salt Lake City: Corporation of the President of the Church of Jesus Christ of Latter-day Saints, 1979), p. 39.

[11]Jerald and Sandra Tanner, *The Changing World of Mormonism* (Chicago: Moody Press, 1980), p. 468. Here we read Brigham Young's account of how the Word of Wisdom originated:

> The first school of the prophets was held in a small room situated over the Prophet Joseph's kitchen. . . . When they assembled together in this room after breakfast, the first they did was to light their pipes . . . and spit all over the room, and as soon as the pipe was out of their mouths a large chew of tobacco would then be taken. . . . This, and the complaints of his wife at having to clean so filthy a floor, made the Prophet think . . . and he inquired of the Lord . . . and the revelation known as the Word of Wisdom was the result.

[12]Joseph Smith, *Doctrine and Covenants* (Salt Lake City: The Church of Jesus Christ of Latter-day Saints, 1979), sect. 84:4-5, 31; sect. 97:19. Also see Smith, *History*, 2:182.

[13]Walter Martin, *The Maze of Mormonism* (Santa Ana: Vision House, 1978), pp. 306-7.

[14]For references to important changes in their history, see Fawn Brodie, *No Man Knows My History: The Life of Joseph Smith* (New York: Alfred A. Knopf, 1971); and Tanner, *The Changing World of Mormonism*.

[15]Smith, *Doctrine and Covenants*, sect. 107:92.

[16]James Talmage, *A Study of the Articles of Faith* (Salt Lake City: The Church of Jesus Christ of Latter-day Saints, 1975), p. 237.

[17]Smith, *History*, 1:368.

[18]*The Holy Bible* (Salt Lake City: The Church of Jesus Christ of Latter-day Saints, 1979), p. 717 of the dictionary section.

[19]Smith, *Doctrine and Covenants*, sect. 73:4.

[20]Tanner, *Changing World*, p. 396.

[21]Smith, *History*, 4:461.

[22]Tanner, *Changing World*, pp. 128-29.

[23]Harry Ropp, *The Mormon Papers* (Downers Grove: InterVarsity Press, 1977), p. 42.

[24]The most provocative recent study of this theory is Howard Davis et al., *Who Really Wrote the Book of Mormon?* (Santa Ana: Vision House, 1977).

[25]Smith, *History*, 1:122-23.

[26]Ropp, *Mormon Papers*, p. 55.

[27]Joseph Smith, *The Pearl of Great Price* (Salt Lake City: The Church of Jesus Christ of Latter-day Saints, 1979), title page.

[28]Transcribed from a tape-recorded interview that Wesley P. Walters and Chris Vlachos held with LeGrand Richards in his office on August 16, 1978.

[29]Ropp, *Mormon Papers*, p. 82.

[30]Ibid., p. 105.

[31]Martin, *The Maze of Mormonism*, p. 161.

[32]Talmage, *Articles of Faith*, p. 466.

[33]*Gospel Principles* (Salt Lake City: The Church of Jesus Christ of Latter-day Saints, 1978), p. 6.

[34]Ropp, *Mormon Papers*, p. 93.

[35]*Gospel Principles*, p. 11.

[36]Charles Crane, *The Bible and Mormon Scriptures Compared* (Joplin, Mo.: College Press, 1976), p. 69.

[37]Brigham Young, *Journal of Discourses*, 1:51. For a photocopy of this and other important Mormon documents see Bob Witte, *Where Does It Say That?* (Safety Harbor, Fla.: Ex-Mormons for Jesus), p. 32c.

[38]Young, *Journal of Discourses*, 8:115. Photocopy in Witte, p. 40c.

[39]Talmage, *Articles of Faith*, p. 39.

[40]Ibid., p. 48.

Chapter 9: Transcendental Meditation

[1]See Maharishi Mahesh Yogi, *Maharishi Mahesh Yogi on the Bhagavad-Gita* (Baltimore: Penguin, 1969), p. 277.

[2]David Haddon, "Science of Creative Intelligence: K-8 Curriculum Option?" *Learning*, September 1975; "New Plant Thrives in a Spiritual Desert," *Christianity Today*, 21 December 1973, pp. 9-12. These articles

discuss the issues raised by public school courses in SCI.

[3]Jack Forem, *Transcendental Meditation* (New York: E. P. Dutton, 1973), p. 204ff.

[4]Jonathan C. Smith, "Psychotherapeutic Effects of Transcendental Meditation with Controls for Expectation of Relief and Daily Sitting," *Journals of Consulting Clinical Psychology*, August 1976, p. 635.

[5]Carmen J. Carsello and James W. Creaser, "Does Transcendental Meditation Training Affect Grades?" *Journal of Applied Psychology*, October 1978, p. 644.

[6]James Hassett, "Caution: Meditation Can Hurt," *Psychology Today*, November 1978, pp. 125-26.

[7]Arnold A. Lazarus, "Psychiatric Problems Precipitated by Transcendental Meditation," *Psychological Reports*, October 1976, p. 601.

[8]Anon., "An English Translation of Transcendental Meditation's Initiatory Puja," Spiritual Counterfeits Project, Berkeley.

[9]Anon., "A Report from the Inside," *Spiritual Counterfeits Projects Newsletter*, August 1976, pp. 2, 4. Information is from an affadavit by Richard D. Scott, ex-TM teacher.

[10]Maharishi, *On the Bhagavad-Gita*, p. 224; emphasis mine.

[11]Ibid., p. 279.

[12]Ibid., p. 226; emphasis mine.

[13]Martin Buber, *Between Man and Man* (New York: Macmillan, 1965), p. 24.

[14]Maharishi, *On the Bhagavad-Gita*, p. 319.

[15]Ibid., pp. 316-17; emphasis mine.

[16]Anon., *TM in Court* (Spiritual Counterfeits Project, Berkeley, 1978), pp. 74-75. This book includes the full text of *Malnak v. Yogi*, 440F. Supp. 1284 (1977).

[17]Maharishi Mahesh Yogi, *Science of Being and Art of Living*, rev. ed. (Los Angeles: International SRM Publications, 1967), p. 271.

[18]Ibid., p. 273.

[19]Ibid., p. 276.

[20]Maharishi Mahesh Yogi, *Meditations of Maharishi Mahesh Yogi* (New York: Bantam Books, 1968), pp. 123-24.

[21]Maharishi, *Science of Being*, p. 273.

[22]Ibid., p. 272.

[23]Ibid., p. 106.

[24]Maharishi, *On the Bhagavad-Gita*, p. 234.

Chapter 10: Unification Church (Moonies)
[1]I am indebted to Jane Day Mook, "The Unification Church," *A.D.*, May 1974, for much of the biographical data.

[2]See "The Candlelit World of Pastor Moon," *Crusade*, September 1974, p. 21.

[3]Hedley Donovan, ed., "Up Front," *People*, 20 October 1975, p. 8.

[4]Bella English, "Putting Heaven on Hold," *New York Post*, 4 March 1981, p. 7.

[5]Quotations from the *Divine Principle* are from the 1973 English edition, a translation from the original Korean. This second edition is different from the first English edition (1966) in a number of areas. Members of the Unification Church contend that the second edition is a text improved in translation, while others cite gross errors of interpretation of prophecy and Scriptures which could not withstand scriptural criticism in the first edition.

[6]Numerous verses and passages conflict with every major tenet within Moon's theology, too many to cover within the scope of this chapter. Consequently only selected verses will be cited for the major points mentioned in the previous section.

[7]John R. W. Stott, *The Authority of the Bible* (InterVarsity Press, 1974) and John Wenham, *Christ and the Bible* (InterVarsity Press, 1972).

[8]From a sermon by Sun Myung Moon at the National Director's Conference, Washington, D.C., 31 January 1974.

[9]This chapter has assumed throughout the truth of Christianity as revealed in the Old and New Testaments. If this assumption is foreign to you or you would like more information to judge for yourself, I recommend reading John R. W. Stott's *Basic Christianity* (InterVarsity Press, 1971).

Chapter 11: The Way

[1]"Power for Abundant Living" promotional materials.

[2]"This Is The Way" promotional materials.

[3]Ibid.

[4]Remarks of H. E. Wierwille, Way Director, at Way rally, quoted by J. L. Williams, *Contemporary Cults* (Burlington, N.C.: New Directions Evangelical Association, n.d.), p. 28.

[5]*Christianity Today*, 20 December 1974. Wierwille's publicity also claims that he studied at Moody Bible Institute, but that school has no record of his enrollment.

[6]*Toledo Blade*, 26 March 1972.

[7]Williams, *Contemporary Cults*, p. 3.

[8]"The How of Door to Door Witnessing" (a Way publication), p. 1.

[9]Interview with former Way follower.

[10]Interview with former Way follower.

[11]*The Way Magazine,* September/October 1977, advertising centerfold.

[12]Total Fitness Institute promotional materials.

[13]Letter from W. H. Elledge, California Bureau of School Approvals, 30 June 1977.

[14]Victor Paul Wierwille, *Power for Abundant Living* (New Knoxville, Ohio: The American Christian Press, 1971), p. 96.

[15]*Time,* 6 September 1971, p. 54.

[16]V. P. Wierwille, *The Word's Way* (New Knoxville, Ohio: The American Christian Press, 1971), p. 26.

[17]Ibid., p. 37.

[18]V. P. Wierwille, *Jesus Christ Is Not God* (New Knoxville, Ohio: The American Christian Press, 1975), book jacket.

[19]Monarchians were quite prevalent in the church in the second and third centuries. In order to preserve the unity of God, they sought to preserve a unitarian rather than trinitarian view of God's divine nature. They were specifically concerned that some people felt that Christians worshiped more gods than one. There were two primary schools of thought in this heresy: the *adoptionists* (who believed that Jesus was an ordinary man adopted by God to fulfill his special calling) and the *dynamic monarchians* (who felt that Jesus was a unique man who was divinely energized by the Holy Spirit to be the Son of God).

[20]Wierwille, *Jesus Christ Is Not God,* pp. 119-20.

[21]Ibid., p. 82.

[22]Ibid., p. 85.

[23]Williams, *Contemporary Cults,* p. 11.

[24]Wierwille, *Jesus Christ Is Not God,* p. 84.

[25]Wierwille, *The Word's Way,* p. 32.

[26]Wierwille, *Jesus Christ Is Not God,* p. 84.

[27]Ibid., pp. 127-28.

[28]Ibid., p. 128.

[29]V. P. Wierwille, *Receiving the Holy Spirit Today* (New Knoxville, Ohio: The American Christian Press, 1972), pp. 4-5.

[30]Wierwille, *Jesus Christ Is Not God,* book jacket.

[31]Ibid., p. 6.

[32]Leon Morris, *The Gospel according to John* (Grand Rapids: Eerdmans, 1971), p. 447.

[33]V. P. Wierwille, *The New Dynamic Church* (New Knoxville, Ohio: The American Christian Press, 1971), p. 90.

[34]Wierwille, *Receiving the Holy Spirit Today,* p. 42.

[35]Wierwille, *The New Dynamic Church,* pp. 122-23.

[36]For an excellent discussion of the gifts of the Spirit, see Charles E. Hum-

mel, *Fire in the Fireplace: Contemporary Charismatic Renewal* (Downers Grove, Ill.: InterVarsity Press, 1978).

[37]V. P. Wierwille, *The Bible Tells Me So* (New Knoxville, Ohio: The American Christian Press, 1971), p. 135.

Reading List

General Information on Cults and New Religions

Bjornstad, James. *Counterfeits at Your Door*. Ventura, Calif.: Regal Books, 1976.

Enroth, Ronald. *The Lure of the Cults*. Rev. ed. Downers Grove, Ill.: InterVarsity Press, 1983.

——————. *Youth, Brainwashing and the Extremist Cults*. Grand Rapids, Mich.: Zondervan, 1977.

Mangalwadi, Vishal. *The World of Gurus*. Mystic, Conn.: Lawrence Verry, 1977.

Martin, Walter. *The Kingdom of the Cults*. Rev. ed. Minneapolis: Bethany House, 1968.

Sire, James W. *Scripture Twisting*. Downers Grove, Ill.: InterVarsity Press, 1980.

——————. *The Universe Next Door: A Basic World View Catalog*. Downers Grove, Ill.: InterVarsity Press, 1976.

Specific Cults and New Religions

Eckankar. *SCP Journal* 3, no. 1 (September 1979). Available from Spiritual Counterfeits Project, P.O. Box 2418, Berkeley, CA 94702.

Hoekema, Anthony. *Jehovah's Witnesses*. Grand Rapids, Mich.: Eerdmans, 1974.

——————. *Mormonism*. Grand Rapids, Mich.: Eerdmans, 1974.

Haddon, David; and Hamilton, Vail. *TM Wants You*. Grand Rapids, Mich.: Baker Book House, 1976.

Martin, Walter; and Klann, Norman H. *Jehovah of the Watchtower*. Minneapolis: Bethany House, 1981.

Miller, W. McElwee. *What Is the Baha'i Faith?* Grand Rapids, Mich.: Eerdmans, 1977.

Morey, Robert A. *How to Answer a Jehovah's Witness*. Minneapolis: Bethany House, 1980.

Ropp, Harry, *The Mormon Papers*. Downers Grove, Ill.: InterVarsity Press, 1977.

Tanner, Jerald; and Tanner, Sandra. *The Changing World of Mormonism.* Evanston, Ill.: Moody Press, 1979.

Yamamoto, J. Isamu. *The Puppet Master: An Inquiry into Sun Myung Moon and the Unification Church.* Downers Grove, Ill.: InterVarsity Press, 1977.

Christian Scripture and Teachings

Balchin, John F. *Understanding Scripture.* Downers Grove, Ill.: InterVarsity Press, 1982.

Crossley, Robert. *The Trinity.* Downers Grove, Ill.: InterVarsity Press, 1977.

Lewis, C. S. *Mere Christianity.* New York: Macmillan, 1964.

Little, Paul E. *Know Why You Believe.* Downers Grove, Ill.: InterVarsity Press, 1968.

Packer, J. I. *God Has Spoken.* Downers Grove, Ill.: InterVarsity Press, 1980.

——————. *Knowing God.* Downers Grove, Ill.: InterVarsity Press, 1973.

Pinnock, Clark. *Reason Enough.* Downers Grove, Ill.: InterVarsity Press, 1980.

Rodgers, Peter. *Knowing Jesus.* Downers Grove, Ill.: InterVarsity Press, 1982.

Sire, James W. *Beginning with God.* Downers Grove, Ill.: InterVarsity Press, 1982.

Sproul, R. C. *Knowing Scripture.* Downers Grove, Ill.: InterVarsity Press, 1977.

Stott, John R. W. *Basic Christianity.* 2d ed. Downers Grove, Ill.: InterVarsity Press, 1971.

——————. *God's Book for God's People.* Downers Grove, Ill.: InterVarsity Press, 1982.

For further information about specific cults and new religions, contact one of these organizations:

Cornerstone
4707 N. Malden
Chicago, IL 60640
312/561-2450

Institute of Contemporary Christianity
P.O. Box A
Oakland, NJ 07436
201/337-0005

Spiritual Counterfeits Project
P.O. Box 2418
Berkeley, CA 94702
415/527-9212

About the Authors

Mark Albrecht, formerly codirector of the Spiritual Counterfeits Project, Berkeley, California, is the author of *Reincarnation* (IVP).

Brooks Alexander is the cofounder of and a researcher for the Spiritual Counterfeits Project.

John Boykin is assistant editor of *The Stanford Magazine* and has presented church seminars and radio talks on the Baha'i Faith.

Ronald Enroth is professor of sociology at Westmont College, Santa Barbara, California, and author of many books including *Youth, Brainwashing and the Extremist Cults* (Zondervan).

Eckart Floether, a member of Rajneesh's group in 1979, is studying at Fuller Theological Seminary.

Kurt Goedelman is the founder of Personal Freedom Outreach, a ministry to cult members.

David Haddon is a free-lance writer specializing in investigating and analyzing cults and new religions.

Joel MacCollam, an Episcopal clergyman and writer, runs a ministry of relief and evangelism to Central America.

LaVonne Neff is an assistant editor at InterVarsity Press.

Woodrow Nichols, formerly a researcher for the Spiritual Counterfeits Project, is editor of *The Pergamum Fifth Column.*

Eric Pement is a writer for *Cornerstone* magazine.

Donald S. Tingle, a minister in the Christian Churches/Churches of Christ, is director of Crossroads, a resource service assisting Christians in understanding people of other faiths.

Wesley Walters, pastor of Marissa Presbyterian Church in Marissa, Illinois, has lectured on cults at several evangelical seminaries.

John Weldon has written several books on cults, the occult and new religious movements, including *The Holistic Healers* (IVP) with Paul and Teri Reisser.

J. Isamu Yamamoto, editor-in-chief and research director for the Spiritual Counterfeits Project, is the author of *The Puppet Master* (IVP) and *Beyond Buddhism* (IVP).